MORE PRAISE FOR

Deer Hunting with Jesus

"**Virtuosic** . . . The populist blogger . . . cut[s] through the hypocritical veneer of elite media liberalism and institutional oppression with the ferocity of a human Sawzall."

—*Houston Chronicle*

"**This recounting of lost lives—of white have-nots in one of our most have-not states—has the power of an old-time Scottish Border ballad.** It is maddening and provocative that the true believers in 'American exceptionalism' and ersatz machismo side with those stepping all over them. Bageant's writing is as lyrical as Nelson Algren's, and if there's a semblance of hope, it's that he catches on with new readers thanks to the alternative media."

—**Studs Terkel**

"**This book is righteous, self-righteous, exhilarating, and aggravating.** By God, it's a raging, hilarious, and profane love song to the great American redneck. As a blue-state man with a red-state childhood, I have been waiting for this book for years. We ignore its message at our peril."

—**Sherman Alexie,** author of *Reservation Blues* and *The Lone Ranger and Tonto Fistfight in Heaven*

"**Should be required reading** for any progressive liberal who wants to create meaningful political change."

—*Seattle Stranger*

Deer Hunting with Jesus

DISPATCHES FROM AMERICA'S CLASS WAR

JOE BAGEANT

THREE RIVERS PRESS • NEW YORK

Published in the United States by Three Rivers Press,
an imprint of the Crown Publishing Group,
a division of Random House, Inc., New York.
www.crownpublishing.com

Three Rivers Press and the Tugboat design are registered
trademarks of Random House, Inc.

Originally published in hardcover in the United States by
Crown Publishers, an imprint of the Crown Publishing Group,
a division of Random House, Inc., New York, in 2007.

Library of Congress Cataloging-in-Publication Data
Bageant, Joe.
   Deer hunting with Jesus : dispatches from America's class
war / Joe Bageant. — 1st ed.
   1. Social classes—United States. 2. United States—Social
conditions—1980– I. Title.
HN90.S6B32 2007
305.50973'09045—dc22   2007001343

ISBN 978-0-307-33937-9

DESIGN BY BARBARA STURMAN

First Paperback Edition

146122990

For Barbara and Ken

A NOTE FROM THE AUTHOR

While the events in this book are true—from "whupping up" on boxing chimpanzees at carnivals to demon wrestling matches in the Holy Roller trailer courts—the names and identifying characteristics of many of the people described have been changed in order to protect their privacy.

CONTENTS

Deer Hunting with Jesus

INTRODUCTION

On the morning of November 2, 2004, millions of Democrats arose to a new order. Smoke from neoconservative campfires hung over all points southward and westward. The hairy fundamentalist Christian hordes, the redneck blue-collar legions, and other cultural Visigoths stirred behind distant battlements. In university towns across the country, in San Francisco, Seattle, and Boulder, in that bluest of blue strongholds, New York City, and in every self-contained, oblivious corner of liberal America where a man or woman can buy a copy of *The Nation* without special-ordering it, Democrats sank into the deepest kind of Prozac-proof depression. What, they wondered, happened out there in the heartland, the iconographic one they'd seen on television and in magazines, the one bright with church spires, grange halls, stock-car races, and community heritage festivals. And why had the working class so plainly voted against their own interests?

Two years later, Democrats regained, for the time being at least, a majority, and liberals have had time to contemplate what they see as the deeply uncultured mob that trounced them in 2004. They have watched panel discussions on PBS. They have argued about where political strategy went wrong. But the one thing the thinking left and urban liberals have not done is tread the soil of the Goth—subject themselves to the unwashed working-class America, to that churchgoing, hunting and fishing, Bud Light–drinking, provincial America. To the people who cannot, and do not care to, locate Iraq or France on a map—assuming they even own an atlas. Few educated liberals will ever find themselves sucking down canned beer at the local dirt track or listening to the preacher explain the infallibility of the Bible on every known topic from biology to the designated-hitter rule or attending awards night at a Christian school or getting drunk to Teddy and the Starlight Ramblers playing C&W at the Eagles Club.

Well, ho ho ho! Welcome to my world!

Here in my hometown, Winchester, Virginia, it is impossible to avoid the America that carried George W. Bush to victory in 2004 (and would again elect someone else just as unsavory even if they turn on Bush like feral dogs in these last days of his attempted imperial reign, even if he is hauled out of the Oval Office in custody). Winchester is one of those southern places where the question of whether Stonewall Jackson had jock itch at the Battle of Chancellorsville still rages right alongside evolution, gun control, abortion, and whether Dale Earnhardt Jr. is half the driver his daddy was. The area is solidly fundamentalist Christian and neoconservative, steeped in the gloomy ultra-Protestant assumption that man is an evil, worthless thing from birth and goes downhill from there. If nothing else, though, Winchester is a marvelous place from which to observe this nation—where the oldest and the newest America and all the vestigial mutant stages in between exist in spittle-flecked living color.

Winchester is foremost a working-class town, despite the yuppie monster-bellums springing up on seven-acre plots all around it and the prettying-up of the old town core as a historic district. You can make lightbulbs at the GE plant, you can make styrene mop buckets at Rubbermaid, or you can "bust cartons," "stack product," and cashier at Wal-Mart and Home Depot. But whatever you do, you're likely to do it as a "team assembler" at a plant or as a cashier standing on a rubber mat with a scanner in your paw. And you're gonna do it for a working-man's wage—for about $16,000 a year if you're a cashier, $26,000 if you're one of those team assemblers. Yet this place from which and about which I am writing could be any of thousands of communities across the United States. It is an unacknowledged parallel world to that of educated urban liberals—the world that blindsided them in November 2004 and the one they will need to come to understand if they are ever to be politically relevant again.

By what authority am I entitled to rant in these pages? None really, other than being the native son of a working America gone downhill. That realization came in 1999, when, after a thirty-year absence, I decided to move back to my hometown and saw the creeping (and creepy) way the lives of my working-class family members, my neighborhood, and my community had been devalued and degraded by the forces against which left-leaning people have always railed—the same forces my family and town so solidly backed in the voting booths.

My part of Winchester, the North End, contains the most hard-core of the town's working-class neighborhoods, where you are more likely to find the $20,000-a-year laborer and the $14,000-a-year fast-food worker. I grew up here, my dad worked at a gas station here, and my mom worked at a since demolished textile mill whose rattling looms were the round-the-clock backdrop of our lives. I smoked my first cigarette here and married a poor white girl from down the street. My forebears are buried here, and all my ghosts are here—the ghosts of 250 years of ancestors, the ghosts of old love affairs, and the ghost of my youth. I know everyone's last name, whose daddy was who, and who boinked whom when we were in high school. So when I moved back after thirty years out West, it was as if my heart was back where it belonged. Which lasted about three months.

It didn't take too many visits to the old neighborhood tavern or to the shabby church I attended as a child to discover that here in this neighborhood in the richest nation on earth folks are having a hard go of it. And it's getting harder. Two in five residents of the North End do not have a high school diploma. Here, nearly everyone over fifty has serious health problems, credit ratings rarely top 500, and alcohol, Jesus, and overeating are the three preferred avenues of escape. These days the neighborhood looks as if it was painted by Edward Hopper, then bleakly populated with gangstas, old men with forty-ounce malt liquor bottles, hardworking single moms, and kids on cheap, busted plastic tricycles. The city government tries to cover the poverty with ordinances that make the local slumlords paint the exteriors of the rentals, but paint can cover only so much.

Wedged between the old railroad station and the Confederate cemetery, the North End neighborhood was once the redneck buffer for white Winchester. Everyone in town knew which streets represented the color line. Those same streets are becoming black and Latino now, and you can see the families who live there going through the same struggles for modest respectability in these rental properties as the working-poor whites who owned them in the fifties and early sixties, when it was possible to buy a house on a low-wage working couple's income. They place foil-covered flowerpots on porches, and they crisply cut the earth along sidewalks with lawn-edging tools, as if the red clay pounded by the feet of neighborhood kids were ever going to produce enough grass to threaten the walkways. They do the very things white working people once did to proclaim: "We might be poor but we ain't coloreds."

Admittedly, my people are a little seedier than most; this is after all the South, albeit the northernmost point of the South. But their needs—affordable health care, a living wage, steady employment, affordable rents, and having some money for retirement—differ from those of all working-class Americans only in degree. There is no sharp dividing line between the working-poor renters in this neighborhood and the working-class homeowners in the treeless T-board-sided modular home suburbs here and everywhere else. The working class here in what they are now calling the "heartland" (all the stuff between the big cities) exists on a continuum ranging from complete insecurity to the not-quite-complete insecurity of having a decent but endangered job. It is a continuum extending from the apathy of the poorest to the hard-edged anger of those with more to lose. Which ain't a lot, brother, when your household income hovers around $30,000 or 35,000 with both people working. Many are working poor but kid themselves that they are middle class—partly out of pride and partly because of the long-running national lie that most Americans are middle class.

Being born lower class in working America makes some of us, probably most of us, class conscious for life. Consequently, a good deal of this book is about class in America, especially the class from which I sprang, the bottom third of Americans constituting the unacknowledged working-class poor: conservative, politically misinformed or oblivious, and patriotic to their own detriment.

Not that I am presently poor. In the course of that circuitous journey between leaving Winchester, penniless and dumber than tree bark, and returning at age fifty-three, a modestly successful journalist and editor, I am now approximately a member of the middle class and one of the liberals at whom I so often poke fun. But a person's roots do not disappear just because he or she managed to narrowly cross the class lines that the American national story line claims do not exist. And what I see is that my people, the working folks in the old neighborhood—though they own more electronic gadgets and newer cars—are faring worse than when I left in quality of life and basic security.

And then there are those who've joined the growing permanent underclass in America. You see them everywhere.

For example, I am standing in the checkout line at one of the most low-rent supermarket chain stores, Food Lion, watching the fellow in front of me, Eddie Coynes, receive his change with nicotine-stained fingers and stuff it into the breast pocket of his shirt. His wife is telling the clerk how her church rallied to buy her and Eddie a secondhand truck after theirs was repossessed: "It needs a spare tire, but we can come up with that."

"Praises be to Him!" exclaims the clerk, as if God had come down with a five-piece band and personally delivered that 1990 Toyota himself. Obviously they are all born-again. The wife grabs up her purchases, a sixer of Diet Pepsi, a carton of Little Debbie cakes, then moves on toward the door.

Behind me are four or five other customers who could be their doubles: overweight, bad teeth, cheap clothing, and looking as though they've been shot at and missed and shit at and hit, each of them with his or her own assortment of money, health, and legal problems. I'm sure of it. I know them. I know which ones cannot get full-time hours at the plant, and I know which one's kid has "a dope problem," as she calls it, and was busted for OxyContin—the poor man's heroin. The clerk is not doing much better; I've seen her make purchases with food stamps as she goes off shift. Every one of them has worked all his or her life and lost ground for the past twenty-five years by Middle American standards. The 20 percent of Winchester who can honestly be called middle class shop at the more upscale Martin's, not here at this end of town, where you cannot buy an avocado or a leek, whole-grain bread or a baguette, or even seltzer water.

When the middle-class citizens of Winchester or of the new suburbs of America—the 20 percent or so of Americans whose lives most closely resemble media images of the middle class— do cross paths with these struggling workers, they do not often recognize them as struggling. That smiling, wise old fellow in the orange vest in the pipe department at the local Home Depot, the one who knows everything there ever was to know about plumbing, is limping around at age sixty-seven on bad knees and has two bone-grafted disks earned through a life in construction labor. He is working solely to purchase heart medicine and the private insurance he must have if he doesn't want to lose to hospital bills the rundown bungalow he and his wife bought in 1964—the one that is now in such a bad neighborhood that only the slumlords ever make an offer for it, but even then not much. He's been losing ground for twenty-five years.

If you had lived his hard working life and had a philosophy of never wanting any handout from the government, you too would be conservative. By "conservative," I do not mean a wild-eyed neocon. I mean that you would be cautious and traditional enough to vote for the man who looks strong enough to keep housing values up, to destroy your unseen enemies abroad, and to give God a voice in national affairs. The problem is that neither the old fellow at Home Depot nor the rest of us are living and working in 1956 and voting for Eisenhower.

The media and politicians used to call people like the man in the orange vest the "traditional working class." They were the ones who came home from the Korean War and proudly built all those 1,100-square-foot faux–Cape Cod aluminum-sided bungalows across America. Now these working people both young and old—mostly whites with only a high school diploma—are nameless (except for the most obviously worst-off, who do have a name: white trash). These are families with two working spouses and a couple of kids who in 2005 were still trying to crack $35,000 and who still make up 24 percent of American workers—at least 35 million by the government's own count.

To be white and poor or just making it is a paradox in America. Whites, especially white males, are supposed to have an advantage they exploit mercilessly. Yet slightly over half of all the poor people in the United States are white. Poor whites outnumber all poor minorities combined. Black poverty consumes a larger percentage of black society, to be sure. But that does not negate the fact that there are at least 19 million poor and working-poor whites and their numbers are growing. (By the way, most poor people work. About half find employment for at least half the year; public assistance accounts for only one-quarter of the income of poor Americans. Beyond that, the distinction between poor and working poor may well be a meaningless moral distinction shaped by the Protestant work ethic. Poor is poor, whether you have to work for your poverty or not.) In fact, as of this writing, according to 2005 Census Bureau data, poor whites are the only group that is both growing in number and getting poorer. Everyone else is pretty much stuck, regardless of the Bush administration's crowing about fractional "rate changes."

Still, the myth of the power of white skin endures, and so does the unspoken belief that if a white person does not succeed, his or her lack of success can be due only to laziness. But just like black and Latino ghetto dwellers, poor and laboring whites live within a dead-end social construction that all but guarantees failure.

Even well-meaning educated liberals have a difficult time with white poverty and semipoverty. If they recognize it, they usually fail to grasp its scale. If they do acknowledge the scale of it, they are often mocked by minority antipoverty groups. The available antipoverty funding that exists is jealously guarded by the groups receiving it; they do not want to see it spread even thinner than it already is. Who can blame them? But are poor whites any better-off than poor blacks? And does the fact that most of the superrich are white help poor whites any more than the fact that most millionaire rappers are black helps poor blacks? Minority advocates can get the "poverty rate" (that ludicrous federal guideline of less-than-subsistence income) of blacks down to 8 percent, or you get the poverty rates of whites up to 24 percent. It doesn't matter a gnat's ass worth because you will still be talking about a raft of folks who are in deep trouble and for whom all the talk about poverty statistics in the world by university researchers does not one iota of good.

Universal access to a decent education, however, would lift the lives of millions over time, especially considering that many of the worst aspects of poverty stem from the intellectual bareness and brutality of the environment. I can remember my father chastising me for reading art books with Rubens's nudes on the cover. "Dirty pictures," he called them. And I can remember my mother asking me if I was queer after I spent a whole day charcoal sketching from Michelangelo's *David*. Never experiencing the life of the mind scars entire families for generations.

My dad was a working man with an eighth-grade education, the same as my mother, who worked in textile mills and garment factories. The whole time I was growing up, I never once considered college until finally, years after I'd left home, the last shudders of Lyndon Johnson's Great Society thrust the opportunity on my class and generation. It is a class thing. If your high-school-dropout daddy busted his ass for small bucks and never read a book and your mama was a waitress, chances are you are not going to grow up to be president of the United States, regardless of what your teacher told you. You are going to be pulling down eight bucks an hour at shift work someplace and praying for overtime to pay the heating bill. And you are going to be pitted against your fellow workers and a hundred new immigrants on the other side of town to hang on to that job. And you are going to draw the inescapable conclusions that it's every man for himself. Solidarity be damned. The much-needed eight bucks comes first.

Meanwhile, if you believe the national story line, all these nameless competing working folks constitute some great American middle class. But the fact is, we are a working-class country. If we define "working class" simply as not having a college degree, then fully three-quarters of all Americans are working class.

"Class," however, is defined not in terms of income or degrees but in terms of power. Especially regarding labor. If you define "working class" in terms of power—bosses who have it and workers who don't—at least 60 percent of America is working class, and the true middle class—the journalists, professionals and semiprofessionals, people in the management class, etc.—are not more than one-third at best. Leaving aside all numbers, "working class" might best be defined like this: You do not have power over your work. You do not control when you work, how much you get paid, how fast you work, or whether you will be cut loose from your job at the first shiver on Wall Street. "Working class" has not a thing to do with the color of your collar and not nearly as much to do with income as most people think, or in many cases even with whether you are self-employed. These days the working class consists of truck drivers, cashiers, electricians, medical technicians, and all sorts of people conditioned by our system *not* to think of themselves as working class. There are no clear lines, which is one reason why the delusion of a middle-class majority persists.

About the only person I know trying to make Americans understand this is economist, writer, and activist Michael Zweig at the State University of New York at Stony Brook. According to Zweig, a truck driver who owns his own rig may or may possibly be a member of the middle class, but a truck driver who works for a shipping company is working class. A self-employed electrical contractor is not a small business person or an entrepreneur. He is a skilled worker whom construction companies refuse to hire because they do not want to pay Social Security or worker's comp or health insurance for employees. Instead, they contract with him, and he assumes the costs of those programs, and takes orders from a manager and shuffles through the farce that he is one of America's ever-growing crop of dynamic, self-employed entrepreneurs. Furthermore, Zweig reminds us, even doctors and professors are losing "control of their work day" (although to earn over a grand a day, most of us would be happy to relinquish quite a bit of control) to HMOs and university administrations, and the "hollowing out of the middle class" promises to make the working class even larger and working people poorer. One can easily imagine the professors going on strike when they are forced to teach classes again, but our self-employed electrical contractor is not about to resist the system, not with Mastercard on his back and a $3,000 Home Depot tab for tool replacement and materials for the next job.

Besides, who is offering to back him up if he resists? Which he has no idea how to go about doing. From my own experience organizing press workers and delivery people at a newspaper, I know that it takes a few outsiders, experienced, educated left-leaning people, to organize local labor in the antiunion regions of this country, if for no other reason than to navigate the complex laws designed to thwart unions. But outsiders—they used to be called agitators—bring something else with them: They bring themselves as models of empowerment. And if they are good at what they do, they bring backbone.

In the days before the spine of the labor movement was crushed, back when you could be a gun owner and a liberal without any conflict, members of the political left supported these workers, stood on the lines taking beatings at the plant gates alongside them. Now there is practically no labor movement, and large numbers on the left are comfortably ensconced in the true middle class, which is only about 20 percent to 30 percent of Americans, as we shall see. From that vantage point, liberals currently view working whites as angry, warmongering bigots, happy pawns of the American empire—which begs the question of how they came to be that way, if they truly are.

Meanwhile, we have what my people see as the "liberal elite," the people still living the American Dream in relative economic safety. Yet the liberal elite—and verily they are an elite group—don't think of themselves as elitists. Overwhelmingly white and college educated, they live among clones of themselves. As far as they know, American life is about money, education, homeownership, and professionally useful friends. How can one blame them? Conditioning is everything, and how could they fail to believe their own experience or what they see every day, all of which suggests that their privileges are natural and deserved?

At the other end of the melanin-and-money meter are blacks. And alongside them are low-earning, uneducated rednecks, bred from generations of low-earning uneducated rednecks, clustered in whole neighborhoods of the same.

The middle class, both liberals and conservatives, are utterly dependent on my people, the great throng of the underpaid, undereducated, and overworked. This is not whining, just a simple statement of fact. We are the reason inflation stays low and the private retirement accounts of the middle class have remained stable. Meanwhile, the working class is left entirely dependent on the Social Security program, which eventually will be slashed and privatized by some backdoor method by the ownership class in order to boost (in a wonderfully self-serving loop) the stock market, which serves primarily the upper middle and upper classes. It is easy for conservatives, who were born into the upper quarter and have never needed entitlement programs, to be against them. For liberals born in that quarter, being against them is only slightly harder, morally speaking. You endorse affirmative action at the cocktail party, then bitch afterward about Shaneesa or Marta leaving streaks on the granite countertops when she wiped up the party slops.

No Democrat or leftie seems to grasp that much of working-class theocrats' eagerness to join the corporatists at putting the liberal yuppies in their place is revenge based. Working-class people can perceive the upper-middle-class snobbery toward them. But that snobbery emerges only when the rough edges of the two worlds rub against each other.

Most of the time the true middle and upper classes are scarcely aware that real working people exist. To wit: It is one helluva comment on the American class system when I can get paid to write and speak publicly about the 45 million or so working Americans who are all around us, citizens of this nation who have been fixing America's cars and paving its streets and waiting on its tables. As a perfectly decent liberal New York City editor told me: "It is as if your people were some sort of exotic, as if you were from Yemen or something."

I don't mean to reinforce the false neocon-generated label of Brie-eating, microbrew-sucking, Volvo-driving wimps. I've done all those things and worse—except for the unaffordable Volvo. Besides, if liberal America has been somewhat too smug of late, my working-class brethren have been downright stupid to be so misled by the likes of Karl Rove, Pat Robertson, and the phony piety of George W. Bush.

The fact is that liberals and working people need each other to survive the growing ecomomic calamity delivered to us by the regime that promised to "run this country like a business." Sooner or later, despite the Democrats' wins in the 2006 midterm elections, the left must genuinely connect face-to-face with Americans who do not necessarily share all of their priorities, and especially with Americans who have not been voting, if the left is ever to be relevant again to working America. If the left is not about class equity, what is it about?

With that in mind, I would like to take the reader someplace closer to the lives of America's homegrown working folks than our media ever ventures, closer to those whose kids' high school trip is to Iraq, who are two paydays away from homelessness yet in their pride cling to the notion that they are middle-class Americans. In what might be viewed as a series of closely linked essays, we start off with a night at Royal Lunch, one of the local taverns, where you will meet Dottie, Dink, and the other good working folks who populate this book. Then it's on to meet some local employees of Rubbermaid and take a hard look at the ways globalism plays out for people in this town. In Chapter 3 we buy a mobile home and in the next chapter we visit the heartland gun culture that few gun control advocates ever set foot in. After our get-together with the inhabitants of the gun culture, it becomes apparent why the antigun forces in America can never win. These Americans love their guns for perfectly legitimate, if not always comforting, cultural reasons that go clear back to that battle-hardened swarm of Calvinist Border Scots who came to America, happy enough to kill off "the feathered and painted godless heathen." Over the past few years we have watched their descendants fighting in Iraq, having their guns and bodies blessed by attending clergy as they go forward to scrub yet another nuisance from the path of democracy and righteousness. To understand why they believe God might want such a thing done, you are invited to read Chapter 5, in which we meet some Christians who want a theocratic state. In Chapter 7 we visit a nearby small town, one of America's many cheap labor and nursing home gulags that nobody is talking about these days, where local karaoke singer Dottie ends up. This opens a can of worms about how married women who work are cheated out of their Social Security dollars and how fake nonprofit hospitals dominate American health care, failing to help uninsured and low-income sick people while spending billions to put small local hospitals out of business and open multimillion-dollar spas and fitness centers. And in the last chapter I try to answer this question: How in the hell can it be that one part of a nation knows so little about the lives of the other? What great illusion in the theater of American life holds us so captive that we cannot even see those around us, much less persuade them not to vote against their own best interests? Or ours. I call this illusion the "American hologram."

This book is written from a changing town in Virginia, but this class of mine, these people—the ones who smell like an ashtray in the checkout line, devour a carton of Little Debbies at a sitting, and praise Jesus for a truck with no spare tire—exist in every state in our nation. Maybe the next time we on the left encounter such seemingly self-screwing, stubborn, God-obsessed folks, we can be open to their trials, understand the complexity of their situation, even have enough solidarity to pop for a cheap retread tire out of our own pockets, simply because that would be a kind thing to do and surely would make the ghosts of Joe Hill, Eleanor Roosevelt, and Mohandas Gandhi smile.

1

American Serfs

INSIDE THE WHITE GHETTO OF THE WORKING POOR

"73 virgins in arab heaven and not a dam one in this bar!"
—Men's room wall, Royal Lunch

Faced with working-class life in towns such as Winchester, I see only one solution: beer. So I sit here at Royal Lunch watching fat Pootie in a T-shirt that reads: ONE MILLION BATTERED WOMEN IN THIS COUNTRY AND I'VE BEEN EATING MINE PLAIN! That this is not considered especially offensive says all you need to know about cultural and gender sensitivity around here. And the fact that Pootie votes, owns guns, and is allowed to purchase hard liquor is something we should all probably be afraid to contemplate. Thankfully, even cheap American beer is a palliative for anxious thought tonight.

Then too, beer is educational and stimulates contemplation. I call it my "learning through drinking" program. Here are some things I have learned at Royal Lunch:

1. Never shack up with a divorced woman who is two house payments behind and swears you are the best sex she ever had.
2. Never eat cocktail weenies out of the urinal, no matter how big the bet gets.

As you can see, learning through drinking is never dull. But when karaoke came to American bars, my hopsy approach to social studies got downright entertaining, especially here where some participants get gussied up for their three weekly minutes of stardom.

Take Dink Lamp over there in the corner, presently dressed like a stubble-faced Waylon Jennings. Dink is fifty-six. His undying claim to fame in this town is not his Waylon imitation, however, which sucks (as do his Keith Whitley and his Travis Tritt). It is that he beat up the boxing chimpanzee at the carnival in 1963. This is a damned hard thing to do because chimpanzees are several times stronger than humans and capable of enough rage that the pugilistic primate wore a steel muzzle. Every good old boy in this place swears Dink pounded that chimpanzee so hard it climbed up the cage bars and refused to come back down and that Dink won a hundred dollars. I don't know. I wasn't there to see it because my good Christian family did not approve of attending such spectacles. One thing is for sure, though: Dink is tough enough to have done it. (To readers who wonder whether people really have names such as Dink and Pootie: Hell, yes! Not only do we have a Dink and a Pootie in Winchester, the town that stars in this book, we also have folks named Gator, Fido, Snooky, and Tumbug—whom we simply call Bug.)

Anyway, with this older crowd of karaoksters from America's busted-up laboring lumpen, you can count on at least one version of "Good-Hearted Woman" or a rendition of "Coal Miner's Daughter," performed with little skill but a lot of beery heart and feeling. And when it comes to heart and feeling, the best in town is a woman named Dottie. Dot is fifty-nine years old, weighs almost three hundred pounds, and sings Patsy Cline nearly as well as Patsy sang Patsy. Dot can sing "Crazy" and any other

Patsy song ever recorded and a few that went unrecorded. She knows Patsy's unrecorded songs because she knew Patsy personally, as did many other people still living here in Winchester, where Patsy Cline grew up. We know things such as the way she was treated by the town's establishment, was called a drunken whore and worse, was snubbed and reviled during her life at every opportunity, and is still sniffed at by the town's business and political classes. But Patsy, who took shit from no one and knew cuss words that would make a Comanche blush and, well, she was one of us. Tough and profane. (Cussing is a form of punctuation to us.) Patsy grew up on our side of the tracks and suffered all the insults life still inflicts on working people here. Hers was a hard life.

Dot's life has been every bit as hard as Patsy's. Harder really, because Dot has lived twice as long as Patsy Cline managed to, and she looks it. By the time my people hit sixty, we look like a bunch of hypertensive red-faced toads in a phlegm-coughing contest. Fact is, we are even unhealthier than we look. Doctors tell us that we have blood in our cholesterol, and the cops tell us there is alcohol in that blood. True to our class, Dottie is disabled by heart trouble, diabetes, and several other diseases. Her blood pressure is so high the doctor thought the pressure device was broken. And she is slowly going blind to boot.

Trouble is, insurance costs her as much as rent. Her old man makes $8 an hour washing cars at a dealership, and if everything goes just right they have about $55 a week left for groceries, gas, and everything else. But if an extra expense as small as $30 comes in, they compensate by not filling one of Dot's prescriptions—or two or three of them—in which case she gets sicker and sicker until they can afford the co-pay to refill the prescriptions again. At fifty-nine, these repeated lapses into vessel-popping high blood pressure and diabetic surges pretty much guarantee that she won't collect Social Security for long after she reaches sixty-three, if she reaches sixty-three. One of these days it will truly be over when the fat lady sings.

Dot started working at thirteen. Married at fifteen. Which is no big deal. Throw in "learned to pick a guitar at age six" and you would be describing half the southerners in my generation and social class. She has cleaned houses and waited tables and paid into Social Security all her life. But for the past three years Dottie has been unable to work because of her health. Dot's congestive heart problems are such that she will barely get through two songs tonight before nearly passing out.

Yet the local Social Security administrators, cold Calvinist hard-asses who treat federal dollars as if they were entirely their own in the name of being responsible with the taxpayers' money, have said repeatedly that Dot is capable of full-time work. To which Dot once replied, "Work? Lady, I cain't walk nor half see. I cain't even get enough breath to sing a song. What the hell kinda work you think I can do? Be a tire stop in a parkin' lot?" Not one to be moved by mere human misery, the administrator had Dot bawling her eyes out before she left that office. In fact, Dottie cries all the time now. Even so, she will sing one, maybe two songs tonight. Then she will get down off the stage with the aid of her cane, be helped into a car, and be driven home.

Although it might seem that my people use the voting booth as an instrument of self-flagellation, the truth is that Dottie would vote for any candidate—black, white, crippled, blind, or crazy—who she thought would actually help her. I know be-cause I have asked her if she would vote for a candidate who wanted a national health care program. "Vote for him? I'd go down on him!" Voter approval does not get much stronger than that.

But no candidate, Republican or Democrat, is going to offer national health care, not the genuine article, although I suspect the Democrats will bandy some phony version next election. If Dot is lucky, a pollster might call her, take her political tempera-ture over the phone to be fed into some computer. But that is about as much contact as our system is willing to have with a three-hundred-pound diabetic woman with a small bird and a husband too depressed to get out of his TV chair other than to piss or stumble off to his car-washing job.

Americans are supposed to be so disgustingly healthy, edu-cated, rich, and happy. But I have seen half-naked Indians in Latin America eating grubs and scrubbing their codpieces on river rocks who were a whole lot happier, and in some cases more cared for by their governments. Once, in Sonora, Mexico, I got very sick among the Sari Indians and needed a doctor. Every Sari Indian had national health care, but the American crapping his guts out behind their shacks, a man who made fifty times their annual income, could not even afford health insurance in his own country because I was a young freelance writer without the protections of a salaried staff position with a newspaper or magazine. Anyway, I wish I could say the Saris also had a native cure for dysentery, but they did not.

It's enough to make you nostalgic for the only two Ameri-can presidents who campaigned for universal health care: Nixon and Johnson. Show me a political party willing to train and put real working-class people on these streets door-to-door, which is what it will take to mobilize the votes of the working screwed, and I will show you one that can begin to kick a hole in that wall between Capitol Hill and the people it is supposed to be serving. But we all know that is not about to happen. Parties do not lead revolutions. They follow them. And then only when forced to. The Democrats began to support the civil rights movement only after the bombings and lynchings and fire hoses and marchers caused enough public outrage to indicate there were probably some votes to be wrung out of the whole sorry spectacle playing out on American TV screens. That was back when a good old-fashioned Watts-type city burn-down could still get Washington's attention. I suspect nowadays it would be one of those national emergencies that Homeland Security would handle.

But Dink and Pootie and Dot are the least likely Americans to ever rise up in revolt. Dissent does not seep deeply enough into America to reach places like Winchester, Virginia. Never has. Yet, unlikely candidates that they are for revolution, they have nonetheless helped fuel a right-wing revolution with their votes—the same right-wing revolution said to be rooted in the culture wars of which neither of them has ever heard.

In the old days class warfare was between the rich and the poor, and that's the kind of class war I can sink my teeth into. These days it is clearly between the educated and the uneducated, which of course does make it a culture war, if that's the way you choose to describe it. But the truth is that nobody is going to reach Dink and Dot or anyone else on this side of town with some elitist jabber about culture wars. It is hard enough reaching them with the plain old fact that the Republicans are the party of the dumb and callous rich. As far as they are concerned, dumb people in our social class have been known to become very rich. Take Bobby Fulk, the realtor we all grew up with. He's dumber than owl shit but now worth several millions. And he still drinks Bud Light and comes into Royal Lunch once in a while. Besides, any one of us here could very well hit the Powerball lottery and become rich like Bobby Fulk.

It's going to be a tough fight for progressives. We are going to have to pick up this piece of roadkill with our bare hands. We are going to have to explain everything about progressivism to the people at Royal Lunch because their working-poor lives have always been successfully contained in cultural ghettos such as Winchester by a combination of God rhetoric, money, cronyism, and the corporate state. It will take a huge effort, because they understand being approximately poor and definitely uneducated and in many respects accept it as their lot. Right down to being sneered at by the Social Security lady. Malcolm X had it straight when he said the first step in revolution is massive education of the people. Without education nothing can change. What my people really need is for someone to say out loud: "Now lookee here, dammit! We are dumber than a sack of hair and should'a got an education so we would have half a notion of what's going on in the world." Someone once told me that and, along with the advice never to mix Mad Dog 20/20 with whiskey, it is the best advice I ever received. But no one in America is about to say such a thing out loud because it sounds elitist. It sounds un-American and undemocratic. It also might get your nose broken in certain venues. In an ersatz democracy maintaining the popular national fiction that everyone is equal, it is impermissible to say that, although we may all have equal constitutional rights, we are not actually equal. It takes genuine education and at least some effort toward self-improvement just to get to the starting line of socioeconomic equality.

Why are my people so impervious to information? Despite how it appears, our mamas did not drop us on our heads. Hell, thanks to our kids, most of us even have the Internet. Still, my faith in the Internet's information democracy wilted when I once suggested to a friend facing eviction that we Google "renter's rights" to learn his options, and watched him type in "rinters kicked out." (Then too, when we bumped into the banner on a site reading JENNIFER LICKS THE HUGE MAN'S SWORD, we both got sidetracked.) Yet two weeks later he had found the neoconservative website NewsMax.com and learned how to bookmark it. Sometimes I think the GOP emits a special pheromone that attracts fools and money.

The lives and intellectual cultures of these, the hardest-working people, are not just stunted by the smallness of the society into which they were born. They are purposefully held in bondage by a local network of moneyed families, bankers, developers, lawyers, and businesspeople in whose interests it is to have a cheap, unquestioning, and compliant labor force paying high rents and big medical bills. They invest in developing such a labor force by not investing (how's that for making money out of thin air!) in the education and quality of life for anyone but their own. Places such as Winchester are, as they say, "investment paradise." That means low taxes, few or no local regulations, no unions, and a chamber of commerce tricked out like a gaggle of hookers, welcoming the new nonunion, air-poisoning factory. "To hell with pollution! We gonna sell some propity, we gonna move some real 'state today, fellas!" Big contractors, realtors, lawyers, everybody gets a slice, except the poorly educated nonunion mooks who will be employed at the local plant at discount rates.

At the same time, and more important, this business cartel controls most elected offices and municipal boards. It also dominates local development and the direction future employment will take. Which makes for some ridiculous civic scenarios: When our town's educators decided to hold a conference on the future employment needs of our youth, the keynote speaker was the CEO of a local rendering plant, Valley Protein, a vast, stinking facility that cooks down roadkill and renders deep fryer fats into the goop they put in animal feed. He got a standing ovation from the school board and all the Main Street pickle vendors, and not a soul in that Best Western events room thought it was ironic.

Meanwhile, the conservative Republicans ballyhoo "personal responsibility" to working-class employees like the guys and gals here at Royal Lunch. Most working people around here believe in the buzz phrase "personal responsibility." Their daddies and mamas taught them to accept responsibility for their actions. They assume responsibility for their lives and don't want a handout from the government. They see accepting public help as a sign of failure and moral weakness. Consequently, they don't like social spending to give people a lift. But self-reliant as they are, what real chance do they have living on wages that do not allow them to accumulate savings? What chance do they have living from paycheck to paycheck, praying there will be no layoffs at J. C. Penney or Toll Brothers Homes or Home Depot?

According to Republican economic mythology, human beings are economic competitors; the marketplace is the new Olympia where "economic man" cavorts; the almighty market is rational and rewards efficiency, thrift, and hard work; and free competition "rationally" selects the more worthy competitor, and thus the wealthy are deserving of their elite status. According to the conservative canon, if you haven't succeeded, it can only be because of your inferiority. Nearly everybody at Royal Lunch feels socially inferior. But in any case, they feel they can at least be self-reliant. They can accept personal responsibility.

We first started hearing about the average Joe needing to take complete responsibility for his condition in life, with no help from the government, during the seventies, when Cold War conservatives Irving Kristol and Norman Podhoretz dubbed themselves "neoconservatives." In doing so, they gave a name to an ultrarightist political strain that passionately hated taxes and welfare of any kind, and that favored a national defense strong enough to dominate any part of the world—or the whole world— at any given time. Neoconservatives hated the counterculture and saw it as the beginning of everything that was wrong with America. And they saw plenty of evidence of a shift toward a welfare state, most notably Lyndon Johnson's Great Society, which for the first time funded school districts, college loans, Head Start,

Medicare, and Medicaid, and cut poverty in half. America was close to being a Communist welfare state, and people had better start taking some personal responsibility, they thundered. We find neoconservatives today all but owning the Republican Party and attempting to axe Social Security and slash unemployment insurance in the name of "personal responsibility."

But what sort of personal responsibility is possible in the neocon environment? A wage earner's only asset is his willingness to give a day's work for a day's pay, the price of which he does not determine. So where does he get the wherewithal to improve his circumstances? He gets that wherewithal from the wages he earns. But in the new neocon environment, that wage does not support savings. It does not support higher education. It only allows the wage earner to survive from paycheck to paycheck, hoping he doesn't lose his job and feeling like a loser down inside. Another beer, please.

Admittedly, a real blue-collar middle class still exists in some places, just as unions still exist. But both are on the ropes like some old pug boxer taking the facial cuts and popping eye capillaries with no referee to come in and stop the carnage. The American bootstrap myth is merely another strap that makes the working poor privately conclude that they must in some way be inferior, given that they cannot seem to apply that myth to their own lives. Hell, Pootie, if immigrants can put together successful businesses of their own, why can't you keep up with your truck payments? Right now, even by the government's spruced-up numbers, one-third of working Americans make less than $9 an hour. A decade from now, five of the ten fastest-growing jobs will be menial, dead-end jokes on the next generation—mainly retail clerks, cashiers, and janitors, according to the Bureau of Labor Statistics.

Some of us were born sons of a toiling god, with the full understanding that life was never meant to be easy and that it comes with more than enough opportunities for personal responsibility. But at least we could always believe that our kids had a chance for a better life. I certainly achieved a better life than my parents. These days, it's harder to believe that. I am quite certain that if I were trying to get into college today with the mediocre grades I made back then, and no family college fund or family home to second-mortgage, I would not make it as far as I have. Years ago, there were college scholarships, loans, and programs out the yin-yang, and a high school education more or less prepared a person for college.

That is not to say the class divide was not a steep and ugly ditch back then. It was. But it is an absolute canyon now, and growing deeper. All you have to do is look back at the unfunded No Child Left Behind program or the scam of "teacher-based accountability." When it became obvious that Johnny is now so dumb that he can't pour piss out of a boot with the instructions on the bottom—assuming he can even read the instructions—the elite regime in power was quick to get up a posse to lynch the school marm, then resume the theft of education funds on behalf of the rich. Conservative leaders understand quite well that education has a liberalizing effect on a society. Presently they are devising methods to smuggle resources to those American madrassas, the Christian fundamentalist schools, a sure way to make the masses even more stupid if ever there was one.

Is it any wonder the Gallup Poll tells us that 48 percent of Americans believe that God spit on his beefy paws and made the universe in seven days? Only 28 percent of Americans believe in evolution. It is no accident that number corresponds roughly to the percentage of Americans with college degrees. So intelligent liberals are advised to save their depression and the good booze for later, when things get worse.

Until those with power and access decide that it's beneficial to truly educate people, and make it possible to get an education without going into crushing debt, then the mutt people here in the heartland will keep on electing dangerous dimwits in cowboy boots. And that means educating everybody, not just the small-town valedictorian or the science nerds who are cherry-picked out of the schools in places like Winchester or more rural areas. These people end up in New York or Houston or Boston—places where they can buy boutique coffees or go to the art cinema—holding down jobs in broadcasting or research or economics.

But what about the rest of the class? What about this latest generation of kids left to suffer the same multigenerational cycle of anti-intellectualism and passivity? Right now there are millions who will be lucky if they are accepted by the military, and if they are extra lucky they will qualify for a vocational school before they are absorbed forever by America's passive, ignorant labor pool culture. In Winchester, for example, even though we are getting an influx of Washington, D.C., suburbanites who feel differently, most native hometown kids are not concerned with upward mobility at all. They could give a rip about school, and they care even less about what educated upscale people think of them.

This is a terrible and silent crisis. Working-class passivity, antipathy to intellect, and belligerence toward the outside world start early. They begin at home and continue in grade school. Yet even if the entire working class in America suddenly got religion and wanted to send every child to college, and if all children made perfect grades and wanted to broaden their worlds, it would be financially impossible under the present system. They have no savings and nothing to borrow against. Many people reading this financed their children's educations with second mortgages. These days, working-class people who own homes have no equity left due to refinancing to pay credit card debt or medical bills. And the working poor have even less of a chance. They rent until they die, with no hope of passing along to their children any accumulated wealth in the form of equity in a home. So over the generations they stay stuck or lose ground. And they stay dumb and drink beer at Royal Lunch and vote Republican because no real liberal voice, the kind that speaks the rock-bottom, undeniable truth, ever enters their lives. Hell, it doesn't even enter liberals' lives these days. But it can. I have on many occasions at this very tavern found an agreeing ear to all of the very arguments made above.

One of the few good things about growing older is that one can remember what appears to have been purposefully erased from the national memory. Fifty years ago, men and women of goodwill agreed that every citizen had the right to health care and to a free and credible education. Manifestation of one's fullest potential was considered a national goal, even by Republicans. Ike wanted national health insurance and so did Nixon. Now both are labeled as unworkable ideas. (Maybe even downright com'nist, Pootie.)

It was to liberal Americans and their party that these humanist ideals were entrusted. To Democrats. To millions who considered themselves progressives with ideals. Nobody kidded themselves that Republicans—the party of business—would look out for the education of the working class, or for the health of working-class children and oldsters, or for anything else other than their own bottom line. That's what Democrats and liberalism stood for: working people and collective progress. Between 1932 and 1980, Democrats held comfortable majorities in both houses of Congress in all but four years (1947–1949 and 1953–1955). You'd think that sometime during those forty-eight years the party of Roosevelt would have done the right thing about health care and education for everyone. Especially during the fat nineties. But the stock market was booming, and middle-class professional and semiprofessional liberals had their diplomas in hand and their student loans paid off. They had jobs and those newly established 401(k)s that begged to be fattened, and airfare to France was cheap and . . . well . . . you know how it is. I cannot point fingers here. I was certainly among them at the time.

So now I sit at Royal Lunch looking out the window at the people on these old streets who not only fail to get what they rightfully deserve but do not even get what they need. Not sustenance. Not a roof over their heads. Not even a touch of mercy, right here in my own town. In Winchester, as in many historic towns in eastern America, the ancient brick veneer hides much poverty. Three-quarters of the town earns less than three-quarters of the national average, and a large portion lives entirely on Social Security. The town has as high a percentage of slum rentals as any big city. Fifty-six percent of residents rent, paying the highest rents, based on income, of any town in the state. Rental housing codes have never been enforced because big landlords and slumlords have constituted a majority on the city council. Over time they have made the town a slumlord's heaven. It's that way not just here but in thousands of small and midsize towns around the nation, each with its own "bad neighborhoods."

When I came back to Winchester in 2001, things were worse than ever. So in 2004 I began raising hell at city council meetings, pulling stunts like presenting the council, in front of television cameras, with dead rats collected from children's bedrooms and hypodermic needles picked up from playgrounds. It had no effect whatsoever. So I gave up trying to embarrass these people and spent the next two years organizing the Winchester Tenants' Board, the state's first tenant union. We did not dare call it a union because *union* is a term so despised in this "right to work" state that nobody would have joined, and the word itself would have made us targets for union-hating and right-wing city and state politicos.

Things were rough. Board members were physically threatened by slumlords and their managers. One landlord pushed me down a flight of stairs, then called the police, alleging I had assaulted his seventy-year-old wife. The cops took one look and figured out what was really going on. Amid all this we were fighting the illegal evictions of renters who joined the Tenants' Board, and we were out on the streets after work serving clients, whether they were members or not. All the elements of a class war were present—a fact not overlooked by the local neoconservatives and right-wing editorial writers, who accused the organizers of attempting to stir up a class war where no class system existed and proclaiming homelessness where none existed.

Well, Mary Golliday was certainly homeless when I first saw her standing in the winter rain—toothless, wrinkled, addled. The manager of a children's store on Main Street called me, asking if the Tenants' Board could do anything for her. In a rare act of enforcement, the city health department had condemned Mary's apartment for general violations. The landlord responded by throwing her into the street and hauling away everything she owned—mostly thrift-store junk—in a dump truck. The two months' rent she had somehow managed to pay in advance had vanished. The landlord didn't give receipts.

Twenty minutes after the call, Mary and I sat together, filling out her tenant case form at the overcrowded Salvation Army shelter. I gave her a pack of Lance peanut-butter crackers, which it turned out she dearly loved and ate every chance she got. Then I called the city sheriff, whose job it is to deal with illegal evictions. Under law, only our city sheriff can conduct an eviction. Listening to Mary's story on the phone, the sheriff replied, "Oh yes, Ms. Golliday. We've had trouble with her before." And that was it.

Mary Golliday had absolutely no recourse here in the town without pity. An illegal eviction in Virginia is a civil matter. She would have to get a lawyer and take the landlord to civil court. This was not very likely to happen, given that she was living on a monthly Social Security check of $500 and change, $400 of which went to rent. Besides that, no lawyer in town would take a tenant case against any landlord. The lawyers drink at the country club with the landlords and make substantial fees in rental real estate transactions. They are on retainer to stymie any court actions against landlords, whether from the city or from a tenant. Nor could I much help Mary Golliday, given that the Tenants' Board had no funds other than my Visa card. And that pitiful little silver joberee was already maxed out from previous efforts on behalf of renters screwed, blued, and tattooed by a system in which property has far more rights than citizens.

Mary's case is by no means unusual, nor is her treatment at the hands of local institutions and agencies, which do almost nothing because they are deliberately underfunded by the city government and are managed by people who understand that their job is to keep costs, and thus services, down. To do something would require raising taxes, and Virginia is a much-ballyhooed low-tax state. The effort within agencies to deny services gets ridiculous at times. A while back an agency downstate decided that an old man living in a camper truck who survived by gathering aluminum cans was a "self-employed businessman in the recycling business" and consequently in no need of aid. In Winchester we have no affordable housing and do nothing for the poor unless the U.S. government pays for it. Churches and, more recently, faith-based initiatives are supposed to take care of all that.

Without trying too hard, you can find millions of Mary Gollidays across this country. The only difference is that here in the South when individuals like Mary are down, we stomp them. The operating Christian principle is that one should always kick people when they are down—it gives them incentive to get up. After that, they can try again to dance to the rhythm tapped out by the invisible hand of the free marketplace. Unless some bleeding-heart liberal is willing to put the tab on his or her Visa card, there will be no justice for the likes of Mary Golliday.

By now we all understand that it was Ronald Reagan's powerful coalition that first turned Mary and her kind out into the streets (except here in the South, where we seldom let them come in off the streets in the first place, instead just writing them off as eccentrics). Remember when welfare mothers were robbing us all blind and driving Cadillacs? Thirty years and a couple of Democratic administrations later, things are only worse. Republicans do not own all the blame. Bill Clinton was more enamored of his own hubris regarding NAFTA and a republic of yuppie mutual-fundsters than of ordinary working Americans, despite the urban folklore surrounding his humble birth in Hope, Arkansas, in 1946. Actually, I shouldn't say "we" all understand how these folks were put on the street, because neither I nor you are what Mary Golliday became after the eviction—a disappeared person. Disappeared until the next brutal survival issue drags her into the sight of society. And all she ever wanted was to eat Lance peanut-butter crackers and watch TV in her own funky bliss.

The misery of folks like Mary Golliday may be a result of national policy, but it is also part of America's one-sided class war being fought at the local level. The problem is that only one side understands that a class war is going on, the side that gets to do the ass kicking. It's like being tied up inside a burlap sack trying to guess who is clobbering you with that baseball bat. Certainly no one here at Royal Lunch has ever heard the term *class war*. And the average construction worker at this tavern certainly does not grasp that the multimillionaire housing developer for whom he gratefully works is one of the people clobbering the burlap sack.

This gives the neoconservative business bloc one hell of an advantage in devising legal and legislative tactics that constitute the mugging of the working class at the grassroots level. To do so, the capos of the corporate syndicates that own Congress use Congress to contract out to the business class in the localities—the local and regional cartels who control city, town, and county governments—the individual muggings of the little people in places like Winchester. The 20 million small business owners of this nation, the "backbone of the republic," Reagan called them. People to be admired, according to the business pages of every newspaper in America.

Like many small-town folks, I started out admiring independent businesspeople. As a teenager I worked in a shoe store downtown and thought it was just about the coolest job in the world, trotting in and out of the stockroom wearing my blue blazer and Bass Weejun penny loafers, waiting on the girls, and combing my hair every five minutes. And I looked up to the owner, Riley Walker, a huge flouncing, old son of a railroad gambler who was deeply scarred by the Great Depression, hated blacks, and was not fond of his employees either. He once grudgingly gave me the afternoon off to get married in a white-trash ceremony across the line in Williamsport, Maryland, the closest place where two know-nothing teenagers could get hitched legally. This old reptile won every civic award the smug Rotarian community had to offer. He stroked the plump leg of any well-heeled matron who could put out fifty bucks for a pair of Naturalizers, fifty bucks being very big money for a pair of women's shoes in those days. He kept the blacks out, his belly tucked in, the blue-hairs happy, and he made a mint grabbing up scads of real estate as he went along. Ultimately, Riley Walker became the biggest local developer of his time; his son and grandson grew the business even bigger. Back then, as today in towns like this one, most of the rich made their dough in real estate because, at least since the Civil War, the land was about the only thing you could make a buck on—that and other people's cheap labor.

Walker's crowning civic achievement, though, was bringing to town a failing Presbyterian college from downstate—conveniently making money at every step in the process—thus becoming the father of higher education in our community. His legacy is a right-wing glorified community college now classified as a "university"—mainly on the grounds of having a southern revisionist history department and a business school named for Harry Flood Byrd, the founder of Virginia's massive resistance movement against school desegregation. Walker's name is all over buildings, walkways, and such, and several little cul-de-sacs in local housing developments bear his children's silly first names. He is one of the patron saints of the business community. The small cartel of southern families that traditionally have run our little banana republic at the top of the Shenandoah Valley, they continue this proud tradition. Today they are raking it in from superheated overdevelopment, leaving the taxpayers stuck in traffic jams and holding the bag for all those new schools that come with development. You can find the same thing in Missouri, Oregon, Iowa, or California—all across this nation.

But the truly dangerous ones are those ankle biters trying to get a bigger piece of the local action. I am not talking about the barber or one-chair beauty shop or the deli owner down the street. I am talking about the realtors, lawyers, and middlemen willing to cooperate in whatever it takes to destroy land-use and zoning codes, bust unions, and generally keep wages low, rents high, and white trash, liberals, and "Afroids" (as one local old-line realtor calls them) down. These second-tier conservative professionals and semipros are dead set on being big players someday. On their way up the ladder they will screw you blind, step in your face, and piss downhill at every step.

They are also dumb as hell. One local businessman returned from a trip to Europe and, knowing that I am a double-bottomed ironclad lefty, brought me a copy of a socialist newspaper. He gave it to me as a joke and said, "Man! Can you believe they actually allow this stuff to be sold over there? Glad we got laws against that crap in this country." I reminded him that the socialist party is probably the largest political party on the planet. "Aw bullshit!" he said. I asked, "Then what the hell do you think is the largest party?" "The Republican Party of course! We're the only country with real political parties." Now this is a guy who has an MBA from one of the South's universities, holds local office, and has influence in local public affairs. It is people like him who stand on the necks of millions of working poor.

My father died with some of those heel marks on his neck. He ran a gas station/garage for a small business man from the late fifties into the late sixties. He was proud of his craft and good at it. Worked six 12-hour days a week lying on his back on wheelies under cars, mucking out grease pits, pumping gas, and living on bologna sandwiches. He never drank. He could never afford to, and anyway he feared a fundamentalist God's revenge on drinkers. He'd give your tail a whuppin' if you stole, and take you all-night fishing on the Shenandoah River. Pop believed Jimmy Hoffa was proof that all unions are crooked, and he loved to eat ice cream straight out of the carton late at night when he got off work. I used to slip downstairs in my pajamas, snuggle up to him, and watch *Gunsmoke*. He had his first heart attack in his late thirties and lived the rest of his life in debt to doctors and hospitals. Until he finally went on Social Security, he never had health insurance. The small business owners my father worked for became quite well-off because of my father's ceaseless efforts to gain friends and customers and do perfect work—for $45 a week. In 1962. He trusted the system and accepted all his troubles as personal failures as he went about his life in our town. The old farts at Royal Lunch remember him with warmth, and more than a few attended his funeral, which is one of the reasons I come to this tavern. My old man had one hell of a funeral, the biggest ever in his church. And I guess that counts for something. I hope so. Because, in the end, that is all he had to show for his passage through this world. As near as I can tell, he believed the small business men who screwed him all his life were actually his friends. His assumption was that businesspeople were somehow smarter, more educated, and more competent than he was, and that the proof was their success.

How on God's green earth did we Americans ever come up with the notion that a bunch of downtown pickle vendors, gasoline retailers, and real estate hotwires are the bedrock of our democracy? That they are an indicator of what is right for America? Well, we didn't, of course. The pickle vendors and the politicians and the corporations that own Congress did. Once it was discovered what a wonderful generator of low-wage, nonunion, disposable, part-time, noninsured jobs these small-time sweatshops were, and that any job counts statistically (even a twenty-hour-a-week job sawing bloated dead sows out of hog farrowing crates for minimum wage, which I actually did for a couple of months), their owners were deemed mighty engines of employment growth. The beating heart of our economy! So now Wall Street soars giddily at the news of thousands being laid off and, "Hi ho! It's off to work we go" at the local Tyson's processing franchise to merrily stab at turkeys for minimum wage alongside the Salvadoran who keeps glancing over his shoulder.

Despite globalism, owners of small and medium-size businesses run much of the heartland. Many of those picturesque towns you whip by on the interstate are small feudal systems ruled by local networks of moneyed families, bankers, developers, lawyers, and merchants. That part of a community's life you cannot see from the road or from your Marriott hotel room, and it certainly does not appear in tourist brochures pushing Winchester's Apple Blossom Festival or the Oktoberfest in your midwestern town. It is in the interest of these well-heeled conservative provincials to maintain a feudal state with low taxes, few or no local regulations, no unions, a cheap school system, and a chamber of commerce with the state senate on its speed dial. At the same time they dominate most elected offices and municipal boards. It seems only natural that these small business owners, after generations of shaving down the soap bars in the back room and soaking the pork chops in water for extra scale weight, would conclude that America is solely about the quickest buck. "Screw the scenic creek, you tree hugger. I'm getting an Outback Steakhouse franchise! Pave it, baby!"

Members of the business class, that legion of little Rotary Club spark plugs, are vital to the American corporate and political machine. They are where the institutionalized rip-off of working-class people by the rich corporations finds its footing at the grassroots level, where they can stymie any increase in the minimum wage or snuff out anything remotely resembling a fair tax structure. Serving on every local governmental body, this mob of Kiwanis and Rotarians has connections. It can get that hundred acres rezoned for Wal-Mart or a sewer line to that two-thousand-unit housing development at taxpayer expense. When it comes to getting things done locally for big business, these folks, with the help of their lawyers, can raise the dead and give eyesight to the blind. They are God's gift to the big nonunion companies and the chip plants looking for a fresh river to piss cadmium into—the right wing's can-do boys. They are so far right they will not even eat the left wing of a chicken.

Nevertheless, there are people in the business class even more right-wing and more dangerous: the *failed* pickle vendors. The millionaire wannabes. Talk about misplaced anger. This guy is pissed off that the gravy boat is never passed toward his end of the table. Take my dittohead friend Buck, who comes into Royal Lunch when he needs to hire a carpenter or house painter who is unaware that getting payment out of Buck is like pulling teeth. Buck sells real estate in this agent-glutted market. He believes in the American Dream as he perceives it, which is entirely in terms of money. He wants that Jaguar, the big house, and the blonde bimbo with basketball-size tits. At age thirty-nine and divorced, he still believes that's what life is about and is convinced he can nail it if he works hard enough. The sports car, the Rolex, McMansion, the works.

In any other era, Buck might have won the game. But not this time. These days the geet is siphoned off long before he sees it, sucked up by the rich sons of Bush oil men and the rest of the new class of financial kingpins. So, unlike our mutual friend developer Mifflin Cooper, who was born with a silver spoon in every orifice, Buck finds that there's no room for him at the trough. He is not part of the old-money Byrd family, which owns our local and regional newspapers, or the Lewis family, which owns our conservative talk radio station. And when, after kissing these people's asses all his life, Buck allows himself to realize that it's never going to happen, he turns nasty, breaks bad on the world. He had the right stuff and deserved to be wealthy, so somebody else must be to blame. It must be the welfare bums. It must be all of those taxes for "social programs for minorities," code for "throwing money at blacks and Mexicans." Or tax-and-spend liberals. Or "big government." It can't possibly be because of the rich elites, because, dammit son, rich is what Buck is trying to be!

I doubt Buck has ever looked at the federal budget to see how much of his taxes, maybe 4 percent at best, goes for what he calls "socialist programs." And he sure as hell never questions the 25 cents of every income tax dollar that goes for interest payments to superrich bondholders. He never questions the cost of nuclear carriers, stealth bombers, and the far-flung legions it takes to maintain the American empire. In fact, he's proud of the empire.

It is possible that Buck is more than willing to let the bond traders and Wall Street investment bankers take first chomp at the fruits of his labor, getting rich at his expense. After all, that's what Buck wants to be able to do, get a bigger bite at the gross somewhere higher up in the food chain. However, real small business and entrepreneurism are becoming a sucker's game in this country, though that does not stop every carpenter, plumber, and electrician in this town from dreaming of his own successful contracting business instead of working as an "independent contractor" for big developers that do not have to pay for benefits. The carpenters and electricians sitting around Royal Lunch tonight are self-employed, part of the building industry scam that subs out everything from framing to sweep-up in order to avoid paying Social Security, worker's compensation, and so forth. The result is all these uninsured one-man construction industry contractors, who hire some alcoholic "employee" or pay a relative under the table to help with the heavy lifting.

To make sure the little guy never becomes a real threat, the current administration again cut funds to the Small Business Administration. Why? Because the real players calling themselves small businesses are not so small at all but are, as I have said, local and regional cartels. They are taken care of. They are big campaign contributors. Politicians know the rules: Be smart and dance with them what brung ya. No need to waste money on a loan to Raynetta Jackson, who successfully raised six kids of her own and is trying to start a day care center, or on Bobby Jenkins, who believes he could operate a pretty good body shop if he only had some startup cash. Instead, tell Raynetta the liberals are going to make all her grandchildren wear condoms to school, and tell Bobby an urban coalition ("urban" being yet another code word for "African American") is going to take his daddy's heirloom gun away from him. Works every time.

Enough drunken reflection. It's an hour before closing time, and if there is one classy thing I do in this life, it is never to be the last customer out of a bar. It took me only forty years to learn that. So I pay up and head for the door, and Carol the bartender calls out, "Get a cab, Bageant!" You're damned straight I'll get a cab. This town has public drunkenness laws and born-again Christian cops who take smug pride in enforcing them. Humble public servants who will throw you against a police car and make your joints scream if you so much as giggle. Then you *will* make the local paper under "Police and Court Notes." No thanks.

Fortunately, the local cab company—which we call "Dial-a-Derelict" because of its halfway-house resident drivers—is next door to Royal Lunch. So you step out the door and wave at the drivers watching for a fare. Usually we know the driver or went to school with one of his or her relatives. And always we can tell by the last name on the cab registration sheet on the visor that the driver is one of us—a fellow link in the chain of this town's common laborers stretching back over two centuries. It feels familiar and good. Sometimes this symbiosis between the wet drunks at Royal Lunch and the dry drunks at the cabstand seems to be the last superbly functioning human thing in this town.

Meanwhile, Dottie's voice can be heard faintly leaking out onto the street: *I'm crazeeeeeeeeeeee, crazy for feeling so lonely, crazy, crazy for feelin' so bluuuuuuuuue.* And those last notes slide away like a silk scarf dropped onto some stairway in the heart. It is so utterly human how all of us—me, the cabby, Dot—get what we need from each other in that moment round midnight when we share the common ghosts of this old town.

2

Republicans by Default

REDNECK PRIDE AND FEAR IN AN AGE OF
OUTSOURCING

On the Rubbermaid loading dock, today's crew is howling like a bunch of striped-assed apes, leaning against the pallets, laughing so hard they gasp for breath. Junie Reese has a pecker pump! It came through the mailroom addressed to him. The picture and words on the box say it all: *Pump it up and keep it up! A top-quality powerful enlarger featuring a 12-inch tube, a pump with pressure-release trigger, and ultra-suction 18-inch pressure hose. Produce extra-strong power with the pistol-grip hand-pump and pull the control to easily release pressure. Powerful bullet adds multi-speed vibrators for ultimate enjoyment.*

"Let's see ya work that ole pistol grip, Junebug!"

Junie is the most-disliked worker on the dock and a company suck-up, always there to rat out fellow workers to the supervisors. Tonight he's getting some of what he deserves. Someone has made payback by mailing him the penis pump box (turns out it didn't even contain a pump, just a nasty note). At thirty-five, red-faced, red-haired Junie Reese has American mutt breeding written all over him, right down to the blurry homemade tattoo on the back of his left hand. ("Is it supposed to be a knife, a sword, a cross, or what, Junie? A 'J' for Junie? Fucked-up-lookin'

J, man!") Yup. The guy is a genuine rope-belted mouth breather of the old school and a bona fide company slut.

Junie's response is to stomp around and barrel-chest his tormentors. Then, when you think it can't get any worse for him, Junie is called into the office. "Mr. Reese, we cannot allow such disturbance during the workday. So I am going to have to ask you not to receive personal packages at work or through the Rubbermaid mailroom. Is that clear?" Junie explains that it was a prank. The supervisor replies, "Just the same, I'm going to have to take note of this, and my warning still applies." Junie nods a *yessir* and leaves, after which the supervisor busts out laughing.

From the highway Rubbermaid's Winchester plant doesn't look very interesting, much less like a slapstick Comedy Central. But once inside, you see that it's a small city, a hermetically sealed culture in which every person is watched and every motion is documented as each cell in the hive strains to produce more and more plastic pails, drain boards, refuse containers, and spatulas. A cell named Miscellaneous One makes small wastebaskets and 11-by-24-inch standup signs that say CAUTION WET FLOOR and can be found in public buildings in half the nations on the globe. Miscellaneous Two makes mop buckets, rubber spoons, and trash-can lids. There is Structural Foam, where carts are made, and Engineered Plastics, the BRUTE department (more on that later).

And then there is Rotational Molding, known as the "salt mines." On Rotational's door is a picture of an arm flexing its muscles, and it is here the toughest men in the plant run the steel behemoths that make yard carts and other large items. In this dark, loud inferno, tons of plastic pellets become molten liquid before they are squirted into injection molds so large as to spit out whole plastic garden sheds at some Rubbermaid plants, though not at this one. The oven doors open, and the carts and containers are yanked off in a relentless rhythm. Rotational Molding is, as they say, "no place for little guys." And little guys are damned happy not to be there. Even humping it on the loading dock beats the iron-man stuff in Rotational.

As often as we hear about U.S. plants moving by the thousands to Mexico, then to China, millions of Americans still labor in manufacturing. And as manufacturing plants go, Rubbermaid has always been considered one of the better places to work. Although it is true that for half a century manufacturers such as Rubbermaid have been operating in heartland places like Virginia to scarf on our cheap, ass-busting, antiunion redneck labor force, plenty of us have prospered under their lights, including me.

In 1967, not long after I got out of the Navy, I worked at Rubbermaid before leaving for life out West in 1969. My wage at Rubbermaid, $1.65 an hour, supported my new young family—my wife, Cindy, and my infant son, Tim. In those days, health insurance at most jobs was free or almost free. I carried my gray steel lunchbox proudly as a family man, and Cindy relished her time with the baby and threw herself into fixing up the first home either of us had ever made on our own. There was dignity in working-class life and family for both of us; we were anxious to prove worthy of adulthood and the world as we knew it.

Thirty-three years later I found myself back in Winchester and close to Rubbermaid workers again. While waiting for my

Oregon house to sell, I spent three months living with thirty-four-year-old Tim, who had been pulling rotating shifts at Rubbermaid for five years. What I saw broke my heart. The working-class world of my son's Rubbermaid friends was so harsh and insecure and barren of the dignity of labor that I damned near cried. Some commuted more than a hundred miles from West Virginia to work, spending four or five hours a day in transit. One vanload of workers commuted almost seven hours a day, taking turns driving while the rest caught what sleep they could. Some slept on couches and in sleeping bags at Tim's when the snow was too deep to drive home, which is often enough when you live in the mountains of West Virginia. Most were family men, some older, others barely out of high school, living in mobile homes or modulars. They were decent and quiet men who always left the place clean, stepped politely out onto the frozen porch to smoke a cigarette, and did not drink. All seemed worried to death about a possible plant move overseas and about bills, medical bills in particular. Their wives worked, yet they barely kept their heads above water.

At the same time, Rubbermaid Winchester appeared to be booming. Overtime was plentiful, and the company had just expanded. So why did these workers look like burned-out zombies for lack of sleep, and why were they unable to break even, even with overtime?

For decades, Virginia has hemorrhaged manufacturing and textile jobs to foreign shores, the flow increasing after NAFTA went into effect in 1994. But long before NAFTA, we had a history of state leadership hiking its skirts and winking at any miserable Yankee sweatshop coming down the pike on its way toward Alabama or Mississippi or Latin America. The big shots make a mint selling property to the northern manufacturers, and the state and local governments make speeches about how many new jobs they delivered.

So it was not too surprising in 2002 when Governor Mark Warner proudly proclaimed that Virginia had "beat out Mexico" in scoring 240 additional Rubbermaid jobs at the 900-employee Newell Rubbermaid Winchester plant. Which meant that our venerable town had consummated 250 years of American progress by beating out the city of Cadereyta, the "broomstick-making capital of Mexico." And in order to knock out Cadereyta—also known for its "pit-cooked hog skin"—the city of Winchester and the state had to cough up about a million dollars to Rubbermaid for "expansion assistance" on its $50 million expansion. A million dollars is a lot to a town like Winchester and not much to Rubbermaid. It was rather like the schoolyard bully giving you a "Dutch rub" on the scalp with his knuckles after already making you hand over your milk money. He does it because he can. At any rate, everyone cheered when the governor indicated that the roadside skirt-hitching was the hallmark of a "business-friendly climate" in Virginia. A Rubbermaid flack remarked on "Winchesterians' dependability and unquestionable work ethic," otherwise known as antiunionism and the willingness to take benefit cuts on the chin and keep grinning.

Now at the risk of sounding culturally chauvinistic, I must say it's darned embarrassing to have to whip the pit-cooked hog-skin capital of Mexico to keep our jobs. As a humanist, I'm glad to see the leveling of the global playing field. After all, Americans, including Winchester's working people, are consuming far

more of the earth's resources than anyone rightly should—
drinking half a gallon of Diet Pepsi from Dukes of Hazzard light-
emitting mugs and yapping on throwaway cell phones or buying
beer can–holding hats with plastic tubing that goes into the
wearer's mouth for $10 at Wal-Mart, wellspring of all strange
and unnecessary purchases. (Indeed, the huge success of Junk-
Mart may be proof that American workers cannot be trusted
with a decent wage. The jury is out.) Still, something tells me
that Newell Rubbermaid is not motivated by a desire to redis-
tribute the world's wealth.

Beyond that, in what can only be called a selfless contribu-
tion to cross-cultural understanding, Rubbermaid brings into the
Winchester plant ever-increasing numbers of what some Anglo
workers call "little brown guys" to work alongside the corpulent,
red-faced natives. Leased from temp agencies, they work for less
and are disposable, expressing their gratitude by disappearing on
command. Contrary to logic, however, few Anglo employees appear openly resentful. "It's what we gotta do to keep plants in
this country and stay competitive. I ain't prejudiced. I got nothing against Mexicans," one employee told me. And so have
others. I can only conclude they are lying through their teeth,
have been indoctrinated by the company, or are so damned dumb
they can barely stand up. My money is on the lying.

Top hourly wages at Rubbermaid now run as high as $15,
up to $32,000 yearly, good money by local standards despite the
fact that its purchasing power has dropped by more than a third
since the day Rubbermaid opened. Forget that fifteen bucks is really eleven bucks or less. Forget that the health insurance costing

$250 a month for one person, with a $1,200 deductible, pays only 80 percent of medical bills. Here in Winchester we have been pistol-whipped into a proper sense of gratitude, so this is considered a good deal.

It is a good deal until you have serious medical problems like Joey Cave, who recently hung up his Rubbermaid goggles for good and is limping over to my table at Royal Lunch to flop down. He is five years younger than me but looks much worse than I do. And I look like hell. Mine is mostly ugliness and fat, but Joey shows the marks of years spent in Winchester's working class. He's been worked half to death, crippled up, then bled for every remaining penny by doctors and lawyers. In other words, he's your average older working factory guy these days. Last year he blew out two lumbar disks (good old L-4 and L-5, cripplers of working folks everywhere, including yours truly), and worker's comp paid the medical and surgical costs.

"But when the doctors said I need a hip transplant too," Joey says, "Rubbermaid said no way. They said it ain't got anything to do with working there, so it ain't covered."

"Well, Joey, I figure you musta worn those hip joints out on the couch, because that's the only other damned place you put in time besides Rubbermaid."

"Yeah, guess so." He smiles. "Cheap couches. They'll kill ya."

Even without the needed hip replacement, Joey is still left holding the bag on six grand. "But hey, I got me a lawyer," he says.

That makes me kind of sad, because I know the lawyer, a local buzzard specializing in such claims. Part of the predatory middle class that swears it is not predatory, the buzzard lawyer, a good Democrat, has lit on the situation and will extract a quick-and-dirty settlement from Rubbermaid, claw off a chunk for legal fees, then fly off leaving Joey with a couple thousand if he is lucky. But until Joey nabs that "big check" from Rubbermaid, one that equals maybe one or two months' take-home pay at his former wage, he lives on $480 a month worker's disability insurance and pays $320 a month rent on a shared house. So if he wants to stop by Royal Lunch two evenings a week for a $2 Schlitz, I say, "Fuckin' aye straight, and let me buy ya one, Joey. Do you need smokes, buddy?"

At one point when writing this book, I decided it would add a splash of the juice of authenticity if I dragged my sorry bones down to Rubbermaid for a shift or two. In the old days all you had to do was park in the lot and walk in and tell the receptionist "I wanna see Joe Bones," or whomever, and somebody—most likely somebody you knew—would hand you a pair of safety goggles and point you in the right direction. Now it's more like cracking a safe. From experience, I can tell you it's almost easier for a writer to get access to the state pen than it is to be allowed to watch working Americans make plastic dishpans on the night shift. In both cases it starts with at least some claim to being part of the print establishment and then "talking to the right man."

From the receptionist at Rubbermaid I learned that the right man was Joe DeZarn, director of marketing communications. Evidently they make him handle the press too. For the hell of it, I Googled DeZarn while waiting for him to answer the phone. First thing up was this specimen of his marketing work for Rubbermaid's BRUTE heavyweight plastic garbage containers:

> The Zen Buddhists focus on The Noble Eightfold Path to Enlightenment, which is comprised of Right View, Right Intention, Right Speech, Right Action, Right Livelihood, Right Effort, Right Mindfulness and Right Concentration. And a very good program it is, if I may venture an opinion. They've been working on this for quite a while, and seem to have gotten the thing figured out.
>
> The real trick comes in when you attempt to apply these guidelines to the more mundane matters of day-to-day existence—refuse containers, for example. You might throw your hands in the air and remark, "How can I worry about refuse containers when I'm busy pursuing enlightenment?" Ah, but that's when the Zen master smiles and thinks to himself, "No enlightenment for you."
>
> The point is that there are NO exceptions to The Noble Eightfold Path, and that means refuse containers, too! So let's explore the Zen of Refuse Containers together. . . .
>
> "Why do the Zen masters choose BRUTE? Because it is the enlightened choice!"

That alone was enough to convince me that Joe DeZarn labors in hell. No matter how much they pay that man, the job cannot be worth it. So I had plenty of sympathy when I called him about an inside look at the plant. "Send me a request in writing," he said in a regionless, full-toned white-man voice straight out of a Merrill Lynch commercial. I crafted my request and mailed it off.

A lifelong friend who works at Rubbermaid, Tom Henderson, warned me that Rubbermaid is "locked down tighter than a dick's hatband. You'll never get in there." After three months of writing letters and playing phone tag with Joe DeZarn—if

writing letters and leaving phone messages that never get an-
swered can be called tag—I concluded that Joe was too deeply
absorbed in Zen reflection on Rubbermaid's "styrene floor mop
bucket/wringer combo" to deal with mere mortal issues such as
those he was hired to handle, and I decided I would simply hang
out with friends who work at Rubbermaid. There is more than
one way to approach those heady climes from which the world's
plastic trash containers and spatulas issue.

"Hey, I warned ja," Tom laughed.

Like so many heartland working-class folks, Tom is a walking contradiction. At fifty-eight, he is a super at Rubbermaid and
the wise old man and mentor of younger workers. He is rangy
and dressed in denim with a huge cowboy belt buckle accenting
his small pot gut (redneck men should never be allowed to ac-
cessorize), and his smile is craggy and wry when he says things
like: "We will win the war on terrorism when we elect a man
with the stones to use our nukes."

Things Tom has done: loaded bombs and missiles at Nha
Trang, where he smoked mucho weed during the Vietnam War;
graduated from a one-year electrical trade school on the GI Bill;
operated his own small construction contracting business for a
few years; got born-again in Christ in 1976 (though it seems to
have worn off quite a bit since). He takes both Jim Beam and the
Republican Party straight up. (About the Jim Beam he says:
"Drunkenness is what God forbids, not drinking.") At work his
radio is locked onto conservative talk shows, and at home he
watches mostly Fox TV. Like many blue-collar people here, Tom
is not completely sure of the difference between the House of
Representatives and the Senate. As he understands democracy,

everyone's opinion is of equal weight, informed or not. He has never been exposed to a union, never taken a college class, and does not expect too much out of life.

"Life is tough," he says. "Suck it in. Don't take chances. Be conservative and stick with what you know."

I have known Tom since 1957, when we were both little hayseeds from out in the sticks, arriving in what is now called middle school in plaid flannel "Monkey Wards" catalog shirts that marked us as poor whites recently removed from our rural estates out in the county. Town and country divisions were much greater back then, before the age of suburbs. Like most Winchester/Frederick County natives, we are "sideways kin." According to genealogical records downtown at the library, Tom and I have common ancestors in this county and town dating back to the 1750s. I wouldn't want to guess about inbreeding in subsequent generations.

After high school we did what kids in our caste did and still do: We went into the military. He went to Nam and I went aboard the aircraft carrier USS *America*, CVA 66. After we were discharged, there was a period when we jammed on guitar together a few times and discovered we had more in common than bad imitations of Bob Dylan. Specifically, that intelligent green herb, which made us sort of hillbilly hipsters, with sensibilities and influences that lay somewhere between Carl Perkins, John Kennedy, and Timothy Leary, if you can imagine that. We dropped acid and "ran women" together, as they used to say around here. Ours was no spiritual or intellectual quest.

Given this shared background, you can imagine my slack-jawed incomprehension when all these years later we meet again and I see that he has become a conservative hard-liner and, at least for a while, a born-again Christian, his zeal for Christ coming in the wake of, or maybe because of, a fifteen-round fight with heroin following the Vietnam War. Evidently he did a little more than use pot over there. But these days the once blond, now graying man sharing a booth with me at Lynette's Triangle Diner ("Square meals since 1948") has the plain old nicotine fidgets: "They don't let you smoke in here anymore. Lynette says the diner is just too damned small to allow smoking. Too hard to clean."

Tom is typical of the ironclad, hard-assed people this valley produces. A couple of years ago he had a heart bypass operation. "At first I didn't feel that much better," he says, "but after I was home a couple of days I said to hell with laying around. So I got a shovel and I dug a ditch and laid pipe for my drainfield. Loosened me right up. What I needed was a good workout."

By the time our country ham steaks and mashed potatoes are delivered, we are on the subject of unions, always a volatile topic down here. Tom is intensely antiunion, which amazes me since I can remember when he had a Che Guevara poster on his apartment wall. You'd think after twenty years in a southern factory a guy would be begging union organizers to sweep through this town like Grant took Richmond. But Tom and most other plant workers here have bought the rightist mantra that goes: "Maybe unions were once valuable, but they have priced American labor completely out of the market. They always want more money for less production." Tom, like me, has heard this line from birth; we know it by heart. He still believes it.

"Whaaaat? How can you be such a corporate advocate?" I ask.

"I'm not a corporate advocate. I'm for the common worker. When unions demand a twenty percent pay raise for the same amount of output and prevent management from firing the screw-offs, it raises the cost of everything. It makes it just that much harder for the average worker in a nonunion job to survive."

In Tom's world, "union workers getting paid forty dollars an hour are not the working man" but are "greedy assholes who drive up the price of American cars so the rest of us can't afford them." Never mind that very few union workers make $40 an hour or that union membership is down to about 12 percent of the American workforce and by no means dictates the price of cars or anything else. It's maddening to talk to Tom on this subject. But when you do, you are talking to the real Joe Six-pack/NASCAR Papa that the media bullshit about.

"Give me one example of a union demanding a twenty percent pay increase for zero productivity growth."

That was a slipup on my part. My people don't cite real facts. They recite what they have absorbed from the atmosphere. Theirs is an intellectual life consisting of things that sound right, a blend of modern folk wisdom, cliché, talk radio, and Christian radio babble. So I know there is no use in pointing out that corporations are very good at increasing productivity using every means available *except* increasing wages and benefits. Or that corporations are beholden to Wall Street, not to the workers, and vastly prefer Asian sweatshops to the bargaining tables of free men and women. In Tom Henderson's world, there are no sweat-shops. "The Asians in the so-called sweatshops working for two dollars a day are the middle class of their economy," he says. A Limbaugh-ism if ever there was one.

I cannot resist: "So you think we all should be reduced to the level of some guy on a sampan in Asia? Is that what you want for Americans?"

"Well pardon me, ole buddy," he replies, poking around in his crumpled cigarette pack for a Camel, "but I don't think anybody in Washington is asking Tom Henderson what he thinks. But the bottom line is that globalization is in our national interests."

It's no wonder Tom cannot distinguish his own political interests. The very language we use to talk about globalization hides its class structure. "National interest" is consistently yapped about in the media without defining exactly who is getting what and how much. So when American workers are told that "the Chinese are taking American jobs," no one points out that the "China threat" is just another global business partnership, one among Chinese elites who supply cheap labor, American capitalists who supply technology, and global capitalists who finance China's exports.

Nor does one talk to Americans like Tom about universal health care or universal education, paid parental leave, affordable housing, unemployment compensation, food stamps, or Head Start. These are shameful "entitlements"—"more damned government giveaways," in Tom's opinion. Frills. "Luxuries we really don't need because we used to get along fine without them. If them people really want it, they will get up off their lazy asses and work for it like I do." Fill in the blanks as to who "them people" are.

One of the slickest things the right ever did was to label necessary social costs as "entitlements." Through thirty years of repetition, the Republicans have managed to associate the term with laziness in Americans' minds. To the ear of hardworking blue-collar and service workers, it means "something for nothing." Undereducated, uninformed, but surely propagandized, these working Americans believe no part of their lives is subsidized in any way. Tom thinks he has never benefited from the commonweal because he has never been on welfare. He is proud never to have utilized any social program. He surely could have used a treatment program for substance abuse, but he found his way out of addiction with a hand from Jesus. Others can do the same.

"It comes down to gumption," Tom says. Child care for single mothers or low-income housing subsidies? "They ain't necessities," he drawls. Our national narrative is about gumption, not giveaways. It's about good guys and bad guys, not social complexities. Weak-willed people and strong people. It's about stories that sound right, political narratives that resonate without much effort or thought.

The current political narratives are constructed by well-paid public relations professionals. Their job is made easy by the fact Tom has neither the time nor the experience to deal with political complexity or with anything else other than his job. The Tom DeLay scandal, the Abramoff scandal, wiretapping citizens without warrants, Republican cronyism, payoffs, charges of election fraud . . . none of it registered. "All politicians are crooks" seems to cover it adequately for Tom and others like him. The main thing is that the narrative be a simple one that makes clear whom to love and whom to hate, who is weak and who is strong. The truth matters far less than the sheer audacity of the story.

Since the days of Ronald Reagan, Republicans have been good at coming up with such stories. Anyone who could sell people on the "trickle down" theory—the notion that working people's best interests reside in giving as much money as possible to the already-rich—is good. Then too, only a subjugated lower class could possibly have bought it. During the Reagan era the Republican myth machine widely circulated the "black-welfare-baby-sleeping-in-the-box-the-color-television-came-in" story. I believed it at the time, and I'm sure Tom did too. Now decades and hundreds of millions of PR dollars later, the overarching conservative Republican narrative has been perfected and is embraced by half of America. Along the Republican road between Lee Atwater and Karl Rove, it evolved into something more brazen and meaner.

At the same time, the Toms of this country were no more equipped to debunk, say, the Kerry Swift-boat story than they were the baby-in-the-color-TV-box story. Even Tom, with direct experience in Nam, prefers to believe that Kerry's open discussion of U.S. war atrocities was an attack on working-class troops in an effort to get the "college-educated vote." This belief in itself bespeaks class resentment of the "spoiled rich Yalie pissing on the fighting man." Forget that Kerry was one of the few Yalies to enlist. By the same token, when George W. Bush illegally wiretapped American citizens, "He did it for a good reason. To stop the terrorists right inside this country," says Tom, adding, "You can't use the Constitution as an excuse for everything."

When Tom stepped back and looked at George Bush and John Kerry, he saw the same thing we all did: "Two guys. One who cuts brush on his ranch and another guy who goes wind-surfing at Martha's Vineyard. Who the hell goes windsurfing?" You can see the answer floating in the air over Tom's head: spoiled rich eastern liberals and their snooty brats. "And by the way," he adds, "why do liberal candidates always take their suit jackets off during election cycles? Who do they think they are fooling?"

"They are fooling the same people who think George Bush really chops brush on his ranch," I answer, realizing that we are getting a bit combative.

"It's lame," he adds, "these white-shirt liberals who do all the sports like windsurfing and climbing up steep rocks for no good reason except to prove that they are capable of working up a sweat."

Tom's stereotyping is born of more than just listening to talk radio. Like tens of millions of other proud-to-be-rednecks, he has neither the time nor the opportunity to read and learn about things because he is so busy working. The fact is that Tom does about twenty-five hours of contracting work after-hours at Rubbermaid each week. Meanwhile, his fellow Rubbermaid workers, friends, and neighbors are pouring their own house foundations, changing their motor oil, or actually cutting the brush the president pretends to clear.

Life is about work for the American redneck. By *redneck*, I mean all kinds of rednecks, not just southern ones, ranging from

Polish and Hungarian stock rednecks of the Appalachian coal country to the Scandinavian ones of the logging Northwest. In the South and the Midwest there are even Jewish rednecks who drive muscle cars and brawl and love country music. For all these people work is an obsession and has been for generations stretching back to the textile mills, the homesteads of the West and Midwest, the immigrant labor mines of West Virginia and Colorado and Montana, the subsistence farms of the South. The forebears of today's rednecks were people for whom not working meant their families would starve. Literally. So the work ethic is burned into their genetic code. (Incidentally, I am not talking about white trash here. I am talking about rednecks, the difference being that rednecks work themselves to death and will never accept a handout. White trash folks do not have the same hang-up.) In the redneck mind, lazy is the worst thing a person can be—worse than dumb, drunk, or mean, worse than being a liar and a jailbird or crazy. The absolute worst thing that a redneck can say about anyone is: "He doesn't want to work," which is generally followed by, "Hell, I don't want to either, but I have to." By the same logic, educated liberals who have time to read, who in fact read so much that they join book clubs, are suspect.

Only one thing can bring such ceaseless activity to rest: a direct hook-up between televised sports and the brain. And even then it often requires vast amounts of beer, which I personally have no problem with, except that all this busyness and beer keeps us stupid and blind to the greater world.

For most working people around here, the world outside Royal Lunch or Rubbermaid or Winchester, Virginia, doesn't exist in any meaningful sense. Sure, there's the trip to Orlando or Branson, Missouri, or Pennsylvania Dutch country, but if you spend your days at a soul-numbing repetitious job, your evenings rotating your tires, rewiring your house, or hauling your aging mother a load of firewood—as Tom did the day after we had that conversation—or recovering on the couch from said job while contemplating the late fees on your credit cards, when are you supposed to find the time or wherewithal to grasp the implications of global warming? You are brain dead, so a couple of evenings a week you stop at Royal Lunch and pour beer on the dead brain. A while back I watched a bar full of people stare at a game of Afghani dead-goat polo in silent, rapt attention. If that isn't brain dead, I don't know what is.

Getting a lousy education, then spending a lifetime pitted against your fellow workers in the gladiatorial theater of the free market economy does not make for optimism or open-mindedness, both hallmarks of liberalism. It makes for a kind of bleak coarseness and inner degradation that allows working people to accept the American empire's wars without a blink.

Like most of conservative Winchester, Tom believes violence can solve foreign political problems. During political discussion around here, it is not uncommon to hear someone talk about the Middle East or some Asian or European country "getting out of line" and "needing to be put in its place." Any day of the week I can easily show you a hundred people who believe we should bomb France (though I doubt many of them could readily find it on a map). For a certain kind of American, it seems, bombing anyone anywhere helps purge some unarticulated inner rage—rage that the easy truisms that once seemed to lend nobility to the dullest of lives are no longer believable. So long as Americans agreed that they were brave and true and exceptional—people toward whom the entire world looked, for example—and so long as they wrapped themselves in the cloak of that self-anointed goodness, their lives had meaning. No insight required. Just add religious faith. Being an American was something to cherish, something worth defending, preferably on the enemy's turf.

So what happens if you are Tom Henderson and you've put in more than twenty years at the plant and let every unique aspect of yourself atrophy so you could do the American Dream by the numbers, only to find that cloak of goodness torn? Twenty years at the same job and the same church, thirty years of good credit, and you look up to find that your wife suffers from chronic depression and that terrorists crashed airplanes into New York. And whispered rumor again has it that Rubbermaid is moving your job to Asia, and television pundits loudly proclaim the impending death of the Social Security system you've been counting on to be there for you, though you'd never admit it openly because, well, it's a handout. An entitlement.

"America didn't used to be this way," Tom laments. "People have fucked up this country." He's not sure who. It certainly wasn't him. But in the harsh new light outside the cloak of goodness there are some very likely suspects, starting with "weirdo university professors, union racketeers, and the rich California ACLU types. People who never worked for a living," he says. "It all started to go to hell during the sixties." So Tom is antiliberal and willing to nuke Tehran.

"Dessert, honey?" the waitress at the Triangle Diner asks. I say no, and Tom and I begin the standard southern wrestling match for the check. I win with the lie that it's deductible for me. On the way to the parking lot, I suggest, "We ought ta get together and play some music, you old fart."

"Man, I ain't picked my guitar up in years."

"I can tell you from experience that you never forget, you just get rusty."

"Okay, maybe we'll do that sometime."

Both of us know that, for more reasons than you can shake a stick at, as the old folks here say, it will never happen. The chasm of time and experience is too great.

Tom and I did not discuss his job at Rubbermaid. The details of being a floor super are not that interesting in print or practice. What haunted me as he spoke was this: Tom is every bit as intelligent as I am. He was a better writer than I was in high school and often said back then that his goal in life was to be a writer, painter, musician. Where did those dreams go? The same place any such dreams go for the children of lower-working-class families. They go out the same door that opportunity for a decent education never walks in through. They vanish along the trails of places like Vietnam or the dusty streets of Iraq. They disappear between high school graduation and the immediate need to earn a living that follows graduation (rednecks are not much for living with mummy and daddy past the age of twelve). It leaves you hardened, and it leaves you standing in the human relations room at Rubbermaid filling out an application to bust yellow wet-floor signs off a hot mold or to work the night shift snaking electrical wire through conduit in a windowless concrete city. And once you've accepted your lot as a citizen of that nocturnal city, you get even harder.

Newell Rubbermaid truly is a city of its own at the edge of Winchester, according to my son and others who work there. Each production department is a sort of neighborhood under the watch of the Rubbermaid police department—plant security—and each has its own drug traffic. Dope in factories is sold by fellow workers, so it is generally more dependable than dope available on the street, because the seller has to face his customers every day. As would be expected in a relentless factory environment, the drugs of choice are methamphetamine, and pot to help get down off the speed. Consequently, piss testing is a fact of working life. Numerous situations require a piss test, including "unusual behavior" but especially accidents. Fail a piss test and you're fired. In the pre-Newell days of Rubbermaid, if you tested positive for drugs, you could keep your job if you went into drug counseling or rehab. Now it's one strike and you are out. Consequently, pot smokers who regularly fail piss tests find themselves moving from job to job—the Dollar General warehouse, General Electric, White House Apple Products—before bottoming out at one of the local family-owned feudal outfits for $5.50 or $6 an hour. And even that last rung on the local employment ladder is usually occupied by someone named Martinez or Delgado.

Back in 1994 Rubbermaid was voted the most-admired American company by *Fortune* magazine. Such yap from the corporate community is tiresome fare, yet Rubbermaid was not entirely undeserving. The company paid a living wage, and, despite corporate management's attraction to cracker labor in the antiunion South, many of its plants in other regions of the country were still unionized. Since its arrival in the 1960s, the company had made a nice return on its investment in Winchester. And eventually, after blacks like the legendary Betty Kilby Fisher hammered at the color barrier erected by Rubbermaid's good-old-boy local management (see *Wit, Will, and Walls* by Betty Kilby Fisher), it was considered a better-than-average place to work by people of both races. Winchester was grateful for Rubbermaid's presence. Plenty of folks my age spent their entire working lives in the plant. Respectable working folks who bought homes retired on its programs and turned back months of sick leave when they departed. By these people's standards, many of the current employees would have been considered Winchester's dregs, people who, in Tom's view, "just drift from job to job." I was itching to reply, "Pushed from job to job, thanks to the new 'flexible labor market,'" but I didn't.

At any rate, just a few years after being hailed as the most-admired company in America, North America's largest plastic products company was a foundering corporation, brought down by the boys from Bentonville, Arkansas. Wal-Mart sells by far the greatest volume of Rubbermaid products of any retail chain. Given such an advantage, in 2001 Wal-Mart's executive management team heavied up on Rubbermaid, demanding ridiculously low prices despite an 80 percent increase in the cost of raw materials and personal pleas by Rubbermaid CEO Joseph Galli. Galli begged. Wal-Mart stood firm.

Later, when Rubbermaid refused to go along with Wal-Mart's utterly unworkable price, Wal-Mart dropped the hammer. It pulled Rubbermaid products off the shelves, replacing them with knockoffs manufactured by Sterilite, a little-known Massachusetts company. Sterilite soared. Rubbermaid dived. After seeing its sales drop 30 percent, Rubbermaid caved.

During those dark days, Newell, which has a slash-and-burn reputation for whipping companies into shape, took the Rubbermaid helm and began dancing to the tune coming out of Bentonville, Arkansas: Lose the U.S. plants. Right, boss! Since January 2001, Rubbermaid has shut down sixty-nine of its four hundred facilities and fired eleven thousand workers, all to accommodate Wal-Mart. At the outset of the shutdowns, C. Mark Healson, equity research director at Associated Trust & Co., stated that Rubbermaid would have to "shift about 50 percent of production to low-cost countries," forcing an estimated closing of 131 Rubbermaid facilities and the firing of twenty thousand workers. Five years later, thanks to the cuts and the addition of the Goody hair care products line, Rubbermaid announced 2006 third-quarter net income of $108.5 million, happily exceeding Wall Street forecasts. At the same time, in October 2006, Newell Rubbermaid conducted a live webcast auction of its 1-million-square-foot Arizona injection molding plant. Bidders from around the world participated via the Internet.

Newell is not the first company to gouge our local labor force or move plants abroad. It's a damned sorry story, one that has become a textbook case for business students everywhere, and an example widely cited by antiglobalists. But the employees at Rubbermaid do not know it. Why bother to keep the toiling riffraff informed? Even if they knew, they probably would not stop shopping at Wal-Mart. Like most Americans, they have never boycotted anything. In their minds, boycotts are for dark-skinned people, a notion that probably has its roots in the lunch counter boycotts of the fifties and sixties. Besides, Wal-Mart is the cheapest store, and they want the lowest prices. And to take advantage of those "everyday low prices," they need to hang on to their jobs. So Rubbermaid employees, in the true spirit of southern Protestant self-worthlessness, being "grateful for the blessings God bestows every day," are grateful to Rubbermaid just for being in town.

As for Cadereyta, the Mexican broomstick capital that Winchester beat out, it too is being devoured by Wal-Mart. America's biggest corporation is now the biggest private employer in Mexico, grossing more money than Mexico's entire tourist industry ($13.5 billion versus $11.8 billion in 2005). What worked in the United States works in Mexico—ever-cheaper goods, lower wages, unions smashed, local businesses ruined. But just like American employees, working mooks down there love those *precios bajos.* They're not complaining. Yet.

Rubbermaid forklift driver Nance Willingham has never heard of Cadereyta. Thirty-three, hillbilly cute, and a single mother raising two kids with the help of her mom, she is qualified to operate a "reach lift" machine—a kind of forklift that can reach twenty feet up and into stacks of pallets. Given the physical rigor of the work, there are relatively few women at Rubbermaid, so the divorced and single women who do work there are the objects of much sexual interest.

Active in her church, Nance does not drink and seldom dates. She is predictably antiunion and antiabortion and is only vaguely aware of NOW (National Organization for Women), which registers in her mind as "a bunch of lesbians out on the West Coast." They are "weird women like the ones on TV a while back, from Single Mothers by Choice. Why would anybody want to have a baby and raise it without a husband on purpose? It's hard enough when you do have one, for Pete's sake!"

Nance is a Republican pretty much by default. She doesn't think of herself as one, but she votes Republican every time. Because of her caste—lower working class, southern, high school educated, fundamentalist Christian—she does not personally know a single registered Democrat. ("I know you," she offered. "That doesn't count," I replied, "because I am a godless commie.")

Inconceivable though it may seem to urban Americans, it is easily possible for many working Americans not to know a person of the liberal persuasion. Why? Partly because most middle-class liberals are uncomfortable being around people like Nance. She lives in a modular home close to the interstate and is raising two kids, one of whom has ADHD, is half black, and was fathered by her ex with a previous wife. She sends her kids to a "Christian academy" on a scholarship. (Fundamentalist Christian schools, which sprang up everywhere after public schools were desegregated in the sixties, are always glad to have a token black to help counter charges of racism.) On Friday nights she feeds the kids a big bag of tortilla chips and cheese dip washed down with Pepsi and calls it supper. It's a family favorite, considered a treat by the kids and a break from cooking for Nance and her mom, who also works (though fewer hours than Nance).

Nance has pride and integrity. She *sirs* and *ma'ams* everyone her own age or older. She has always had a job, has never taken a penny from her parents, and has paid her bills on time since she graduated from high school. Her mom says, "Once in high school she put a skirt and jacket on layaway at a store where she worked during the Christmas season. It was slow season, so they laid her off way early. That girl gathered aluminum cans in the freezing snow to make the weekly payments."

Nance's political and cultural world is entirely defined by media of the lowest and broadest common denominator, by her church, and by her workplace. Especially her workplace. When it comes to plants like Rubbermaid and the folks who work in them, you are talking about millions of people who are not on political mailing lists, couldn't care less what is on the Internet, and would not know a BlackBerry from a garage-door opener. They spend eight hours a day listening to talk radio through earphones as they work. And they are aware of the politics of their supervisors and bosses.

It would be wrong to say that supervisors put pressure on workers like Nance to vote conservative. They don't have to. They merely let their politics be known, and the desire to curry favor with the boss does the rest. In this work environment employees suck up reflexively. Consequently, people like Nance listen closely to the alpha-male supervisor in the break room for clues about opinions they should and should not hold or express—not only about politics but also about anything else that might go against the grain in the plant environment. Naturally, there is the ever-present antiunion pressure. From the first employee training and indoctrination sessions, Newell Rubbermaid makes the corporate position clear. This is not really necessary. We learned the lesson as kids. I remember my ninth-grade history teacher at Handley High School spending an entire classroom hour on "communist labor unions." The same teacher, rest his soul, also told us that "coloreds are happy enough to have a coon tail on their car antennas and a plate of fried chicken on their table."

Meanwhile, inside the radio headphones of Nance and everyone else allowed to tune in while working at Rubbermaid, talk radio squawks, honks, and howls indignantly about the state of the Republic. The rants of Rush Limbaugh, Gordon Liddy, Michael Reagan, and other right-wing talk jocks are interspersed with debt consolidation commercials. "Sometimes I listen to contemporary Christian stations, but they play the same thing over and over and over," explains Nance. So she keeps drifting back to talk radio (*"Today our guest is John Lee Clary, former Ku Klux Klansman now ministering for our Lord and Savior. His new book is named* From Klan to Christ! *Good morning, John!"*) and sometimes local modern country stations, where ultraconservatism is a given. The politically indifferent and nonreligious listen to classic rock.

It is safe to say that radio supplies the workers with most of their knowledge of things political. Most do not subscribe to a newspaper, and the political influence of their favorite network, Fox, is somewhat overrated out here—except in the hypnagogic sense, which is admittedly no small thing. But that intimate radio space that fills the void of shift work . . . ahhh! If you've ever done "eight straight" cutting tabs off molded plastic or stacking pallets, you know how powerful the sound of the relentless "one voice speaking to the many" is to those working in headphone radio space, that bubble of radio reality within the roaring of machines. For eight hours it is a voice inside your head that sounds like your own voice. Ask any assembly-line worker, night janitor, or house painter.

Still, none of the above is the core reason why Nance votes Republican. Organized as the hard right-wing putsch has been, its success among working people is due as much to widespread misconceptions about what is going wrong with America as it is due to any master plan devised by the New Conservatism, though neoconservative planning has played its part. The New Conservatism arose in the same way left-wing movements do, by approximately the same process, and for the same reasons: widespread but unacknowledged dissatisfaction, in this case with the erosion of "traditional" life and values in America as working people perceived them. Otherwise known as change. Unease had been growing for decades before the Republican Revolution of 1994; it has been the backdrop to Nance's entire life. When the Republicans gave it a name and a nail to hang upon, people like Nance, Tom, Poot, and the rest stepped forward to claim it.

There is no good reason why for the past thirty years the uncertainty and dissatisfaction of people like Tom and Nance was automatically snubbed as unenlightened by so many on the left. If the left had identified and dealt with this dissatisfaction early on, if they had counteracted the fallacies the Republicans used to explain that dissatisfaction, if they had listened instead of stereotyping blue-collar angst as "Archie Bunkerism" (itself a stereotype of a stereotype delivered unto their minds by television) and maybe offered some gutsy, comprehensible, and practical solutions, we might have witnessed something better than the Republican syndicate's lying and looting of the past six years. Real movements take advantage of the protest-potential to be found among dissatisfied and disappointed people—people disenfranchised by bureaucracy, technocracy, and "experts." Rightists tapped into that dissatisfaction by lamenting the loss of community and values and attributing it to the "cultural left's" feminism and antiracism, the gay movement, and so on. The Republican message, baloney though it is, was accessible to Nance. The Democrats didn't have any message at all.

As it stands now, Nance has no political leadership whatsoever. Nobody stands up for the interests of people like her unless a few of them get crushed under a seam of coal, thereby providing the required emotional grist for the nightly news. Only right-wing politicians appealing to their religious prejudices and ignorance on behalf of big money pay any attention to them. If you hang around real working-class places very long, whether it be the young folks' Ruby Tuesdays at the Apple Blossom Mall or the old guys' Royal Lunch down by the tracks, you'll see that decent working folks seldom talk politics or current events except during the final weeks before an election and when prompted by lefty agitators like me or grassroots neocon Republican operatives—people who understand that the four cornerstones of the American political psyche are (1) emotion substituted for thought, (2) fear, (3) ignorance, and (4) propaganda.

When the United States attacked Iraq, there was a mood swing at Royal Lunch, an occasional brief mention of the war but no real discussion of it. The middle-class white professional's fern-and-pale-ale joints downtown were all fired up for the war their president had launched. But at Royal Lunch, as usual, discussion revolved around sports, movies, where to get good ribs and seafood, and why GM can't seem to build a good engine. Not exactly amazing, given that our national reality is television. Nothing else holds us together politically except fear, and even that is generated through our TV sets. So when television's one voice tells the many to support the troops, we say to ourselves, "That sounds like the right thing to do," and we write mental notes to ourselves saying, "Support our troops." Then we have a beer. As I've said, the intellectual lives of most working-class Americans consist of things that sound as if they might be true, and that is why millions are spent on sound bites and sloganeering.

To the extent that we can be said to hold beliefs, we hold the beliefs we think we are expected to hold. Just as we hold little American flags and put magnetic ribbons on our cars to tell others who we believe we are: Americans and Americans only. Plain Americans, isolated from the rest of the world by the certainty that it's better to be American than anything else, even if we really can't prove why. Even if we are one house payment away from homelessness, even if our kids can't read and our asses are getting so big they have their own zip codes, it's comforting to know we are at least in the best place on earth. There is America, and there is the rest of the world—envious and plotting to bring us down and "steal our freedom."

Enter the shit stirrers or, more politely, political activists such as Laurita Barr. Many of the entrenched bad attitudes that Internet liberals attribute to "memes" are simply the work of these wicked messengers—nothing more than lies sold at the retail level, best countered at the grassroots level where they are distributed. In towns like Winchester, you can more easily see the grassroots workings of far-right politics in bars, clubs, and fraternal organizations than by monitoring blogs or newspapers. One thing I have noticed is that Republicans' everyday lives seem naturally woven into the fabric of the community in a way that the everyday lives of the left have not been since the Great Depression and the social justice movements of the sixties. Despite the class system of these towns, many rich Republicans still meet the small business class and working class on their own turf. And working-class people encounter Republicans face-to-face at churches, all-you-can-eat spaghetti fund-raisers, fraternal organizations like the Elks Club, and local small businesses. The Republican ideals of old have always had a solid lock in the heartland, and all that proximity can lead to identification.

Consequently, on an evening like this one you find people like Laurita Barr drinking a few beers with the proles at the tavern: Mac the house painter; Rubbermaid second-shift workers Tom and Nance (who usually drinks one Diet Coke, then leaves); plus a couple of others who pull chairs up near the table to hear the great lady's thoughts. Just sitting at her table is, to them, a social honor, one big enough that Nance might even stay and have two Diet Cokes tonight. Laurita is one of the town's bigger—but by no means biggest—landlords, with two or three hundred residential units, many of them in the blighted North End. And she is of course a realtor.

Laurita, age fifty, wears sharp business suits during the day and sports Max Studio and Nordy's casual afterwork wear in Royal Lunch. She is a millionaire several times over, and she runs the family real estate and rental business like a machine. "I do not fool around. The eviction process begins the minute they are late enough on rent to start the paperwork," she says, taking a sip of Sam Adams. She is a twenty-four-hour-a-day Republican operative and enforcer. Along with her ceaseless activism in city hall against tenants' rights and property taxes (houses converted to multiunit slum properties here pay the same taxes as single-family dwellings, despite the strains they put on city services), she also spends some bar time bad-mouthing progressive politics and anything remotely related to the Democratic Party. Which is what she is doing on this particular June evening.

Laurita can make hay out of anything. The *Winchester Star* has been running a story about a local woman who got twenty years for giving pornographic photos of her thirteen-year-old daughter to her husband, who is in prison for abusing the daughter. The porno woman's picture is plastered on the front page at every opportunity the editors can think up. Hers is a face straight out of a Dorothea Lange dust-bowl photo. The gusto with which Winchester enjoys such a spectacle is a reminder that our town was founded amid a welter of public dunkings, floggings, and witchcraft charges. Salem was not alone in that dark superstitious era. The Yankees, however, seem to have gotten beyond it.

Laurita is exhorting the drinkers at her table: "This is beyond disgusting! A woman who takes pornographic photos of her thirteen-year-old daughter for her own husband in prison who had abused the same girl! I would bet money that the ACLU comes to her rescue. She's just the kind of person liberals and Democrats champion." Laurita pronounces the word *liberal* with contempt. When a less biased voice points out that she may be going a bit overboard, she says: "Ever hear of NAMBLA (North American Man Boy Love Association)? They had a seat at the Democratic convention in 2000. Official delegates. Boy Scouts were booed at the convention but NAMBLA got seated. Dems, liberals, they are all the same."

"So, where did you hear about the Boys Scouts being booed by the national Democrats?" asks Tom, who I believe has a Boy Scout grandson.

"The Scout district commissioner brought it up at our meeting," says Laurita. (Later I Googled this piece of information. The only reference I could find was on two conservative websites, NewsMax.com and FreeRepublic.com, which mirrored her remarks right down to "I heard it at a troop meeting from a district commissioner.") Laurita adds, "The Democrats are trying to brand the Scouts as a hate group."

Looking around the two tables pushed together, I can see that people seem a little disturbed. No one questions Laurita's veracity because of her social and economic status. In the American provinces, especially the southern ones, wealth is proof of God's love and bestows the power to mess over anyone who disagrees with you. Even putting this aside, it seems prudent to

Nance, I'm sure, to avoid any political party that considers the Boy Scouts a hate group. I see this very kind of thing happen nearly every day on local Internet forums and bulletin boards. In a very real sense this is Internet-driven Republican outreach, something for which there is no meaningful liberal equivalent. Robust as the Democratic blogosphere is, Democrats seem less inclined than Republicans to run downtown and spread the word in person. Perhaps they simply do not have as many party operatives at the grassroots level. Perhaps they do not have the same strong self-interest at stake as Laurita, whose real estate taxes and income are so directly affected by the party in power. In any case, coupled with GOP hate talk radio all day, the network of GOP operatives creates a powerful propaganda double whammy.

The key is misrepresentation and guilt by association. A good example is using the old saw of "less government" to associate presumed government inefficiency with Social Security. Rather than abolish Social Security outright—which the right knows cannot be done because it remains the most popular government program ever created—the neoconservatives recommend privatizing it to make it more efficient and increase returns on retirees' investments. Or as Tom says, "Let the pros on Wall Street handle it. Everybody knows how wasteful and inefficient governmental bureaucracies are." The truth is something that conservatives will never admit: The administrative costs of Social Security are far lower than the administrative costs of any private sector company, only 3.5 percent of its annual budget, according to the Government Accounting Office. But in tying Social Security to the notion of government waste, conservatives translate the issue into terms that the ordinary Joe who spends forty bucks and most of a day at the DMV trying to get a postage stamp–size license plate sticker can understand.

To spread its message, the GOP has a huge number of grassroots operatives. They turn up everywhere—at city council meetings and in the letters columns of local newspapers. Whenever they spot an opportunity to inject a slogan or recite some conservative rhetoric or retail a concocted story from NewsMax, Town-Hall, or FrontPage, they take it. That's why the GOP has such a unified response to any liberal message.

The nationwide grassroots network of zealous conservatives such as Laurita recruits manpower for the entire GOP. At the humble level of the small towns, local candidates are raised and groomed for state and national office, backed by a host of Lauritas contributing and working the crowds and writing letters to the editor. And it is from these local grassroots GOP business-based cartels that the army of campaign volunteers, political activists, and spokesmen springs. The result is that, even though the social and economic visions of the ultrarightists are repulsive, the rightists succeed at forcing their vision of America down our throats because they have committed themselves to organization and communication. They had a setback in 2006, and they may have more setbacks in 2008, but they are dedicated to victory at any cost.

Liberals, in contrast, chatter among themselves online or at social gatherings and make little attempt to engage, much less convert, the heathen tribes. Eventually they will have to come out here into the real world and stroke guys like ole Pootie for his vote, an unpleasant job if ever there was one. I'm sure he'll enjoy the attention.

Meanwhile, regardless of the 2006 midterm victories, shit stirring is still working for Laurita and still works for the Republicans here. It doesn't work for me, which is why Laurita and I are sworn enemies. Enemies enough to leave Royal Lunch when the other walks in, although sometimes we both stay if we happen to be drunk enough to be looking for a good fight.

Of course, all the Republican shit stirring in the world would be useless if there were no working-class anger or anxiety to be tapped. Working folks may not spend much time mouthing off about politics, but many sure as hell fester inside about their lives and livelihoods. And many, if not most, working-class people around this town feel a deep anger that has very little to do with the issues ballyhooed by their political and religious leaders. They are not especially exercised about *Queer Eye for the Straight Guy* or the sacrifice of unborn children, though if you ask them they will certainly find both unpalatable. The source of their anger is more fundamental. It's the daily insults they suffer from their employers, from their government, and from more educated fellow Americans—the doctors, lawyers, journalists, academicians, and others who quietly disdain working folks.

The seemingly hateful values that many working people display when it comes to sexuality and race are not rooted in any inherent malevolence. The Tom Henderson who once loved to play folk guitar on the porch at night did not mutate into the iron heart he is today of his own volition. Nam did part of it; the increasing brutality of the American workplace and being pitted against every other working American did most of the rest. Tom was strong enough to beat heroin but no match against the increasing meanness at the heart of our Republic, for which his youth was vaporized in the face of war. The tide of our national meanness rises incrementally, one brutalizing experience at a time, inside one person at a time in a chain of working-class Americans stretching back for decades. Back to the terror-filled nineteen-year-old girl from Weirton, West Virginia, who patrols the sweat-smelling halls of one of the empire's far-flung prisons at midnight. Back to my neighbor's eighty-year-old father, who remembers getting paid $2 apiece for literally cracking open the heads of union organizers at our textile and sewing mills during the days of Virginia's Byrd political machine. (It was the Depression and the old man needed the money to support his family.) The brutal way in which America's hardest-working folks historically were forced to internalize the values of a gangster capitalist class continues to elude the left, which, with few exceptions, understands not a thing about how this political and economic system has hammered the humanity of ordinary working people.

Much of the ongoing battle for America's soul is about healing the souls of these Americans and rousing them from the stupefying glut of commodity and spectacle. It is about making sure that they—and we—refuse to accept torture as the act of "heroes" and babies deformed by depleted uranium as the "price of freedom." Caught up in the great self-referential hologram of imperial America, force-fed goods and hubris like fattened steers, working people like World Championship Wrestling and Confederate flags and flat-screen televisions and the idea of an American empire. ("American Empire! I like the sound of that!" they think to themselves, without even the slightest idea what it means historically.)

"The people" doing our hardest work and fighting our wars are not altruistic and probably never were. They don't give a rat's bunghole about the world's poor or the planet or animals or anything else. Not really. "The people" like cheap gas. They like chasing post–Thanksgiving Day Christmas sales. And if fascism comes, they will like that too if the cost of gas isn't too high and Comcast comes through with a twenty-four-hour NFL channel.

That is the American hologram. That is the peculiar illusion we live within, the illusion that holds us together, makes us alike, yet tells each of us we are unique. And it will remain in force until the whole shiteree comes down around our heads. Working people do not deny reality. They create it from the depths of their perverse ignorance, even as the so-called left speaks in non sequiturs and wonders why it cannot gain any political traction. Meanwhile, for the people, it is football and NASCAR and a republic free from married queers and trigger locks on guns. That's what they voted for—an armed and moral republic. And that's what we get when we stand by and watch the humanity get hammered out of our fellow citizens, letting them be worked cheap and farmed like a human crop for profit.

Genuine moral values have jack to do with politics. But in an obsessively religious nation, values remain the most effective smoke screen for larceny by the rich and hatred and fear by the rest. What Christians and so many quiet, ordinary Americans were voting for in the presidential elections of 2000 and 2004 was fear of human beings culturally unlike themselves, particularly gays and lesbians and Muslims and other non-Christians. That's why in eleven states Republicans got constitutional amendments banning same-sex marriage on the ballot. In nine of them the bill passed easily. It was always about fearing and, in the worst cases, hating "the other."

Being a southerner, I have hated in my lifetime. I can remember schoolyard discussions of supposed "nigger knifing" of white boys at night and such. And like most people over fifty, it shows in my face, because by that age we have the faces we deserve. Likewise I have seen hate in others and know it when I see it. And I am seeing more of it now than ever before in my lifetime, which is saying something considering that I grew up down here during the Jim Crow era. Fanned and nurtured by neoconservative elements, the hate is every bit equal to the kind I saw in my people during those violent years. Irrational. Deeply rooted. Based on inchoate fears.

The fear is particularly prevalent in the middle and upper-middle classes here, the very ones most openly vehement about being against using the words *nigger* and *fuck*. They are what passes for educated people in a place like Winchester. You can smell their fear. Fear of losing their advantages and money. Fear there won't be enough time to grab and stash enough geet to keep themselves and their offspring in Chardonnay and farting through silk for the next fifty years. So they keep the lie machinery and the smoke generators cranking full blast as long as possible, hoping to elect another one of their own kind to the White House—Democratic or Republican, it doesn't matter so long as they keep the scam going. The Laurita Barrs speak in knowing, authoritative tones, and the inwardly fearful house painter and single-mom forklift driver listen and nod. Why take a chance on voting for a party that would let homos be scout masters?

* * *

During Christmas week in 2005, the neocon grassroots network was humming along. Two days before Christmas, a Republican operative named Ted was vigorously circulating on Winchester Internet forums a bogus Republican Christmas story:

Democrat Landlord Bilks Republican's Homeless Shelter

A liberal lawyer in Los Angeles has thrown nearly three dozen homeless center residents back on the streets because of something he finds indefensible: The center's founder is a Republican and voted for President Bush. . . .

According to the story, some thirty men, women, and children were forced into the streets by the heartless liberal Democrat, a wicked landlord and a lawyer to boot, who jacked up the rent from $2,500 per month to $18,333 per month. The shelter operator, a fellow named Ted Hayes, allegedly "forsook a middle-class lifestyle years ago to live on the streets" and give succor to the homeless. He is a bit too conveniently quoted as saying "I support President Bush, and I support the Republican Party." Near the end of the story, we find the one final bit of gilt added to the lily, Hayes is black.

That's the thing about the neocon smoke-and-lie machine. It's relentless. It just never lets up. Not even at Christmas.

Thirty years ago the Lauritas and the Teds of Winchester and red-state America were doing the same thing—leading the Nances and Toms around by their noses. It's a class system, and members of Laurita's class are issued silver-plated nose hooks at birth. Their relationships with each other and with the world are the same as when they were in high school. We knew damned well who was going to work at the Rubbermaids and who was going to work on the fruit-packing lines. Everyone still occupies the same niche in the small-town caste system (even though we are now more of a small city), and everyone still sees the world from his or her small berth in that limited system. New York City is still seen as a crime-ridden hell into which no sane person would set foot. France is the land of gutless, pussy-eating "Frogs."

Most disturbingly, the Iraq War, despite all the noise, is at this writing in 2006 a distant thing that occasionally spits a coffin in our direction containing some local working-class son or daughter. The flag-draped box is shown on the front page of the local paper, everyone salutes and remarks on how sad it is, but really nobody but the soldier's family and church gives a hoot. They really don't. You can see it in their eyes. The new Washington Nationals baseball franchise over in D.C. gets far, far more discussion than the war, dead locals or no dead locals. It is one of the hologram's biggest media myths that small towns are thrown into deep mourning when one of their young is killed in Iraq. There was a time when that would have been true, but long ago our lives were numbed by the money grind and by the birth-to-death drenching in marketing and messages and sports spectacle, by the complete absence of genuine public questioning of the notion that America is the best nation on earth, superior in all things and therefore unassailable. Consequently, there is growing dissatisfaction with the war, but, in this town at least, it is because we are not winning, not because of the dead.

A community that has become so numb that it no longer mourns its own dead cannot be called a community, and certainly cannot be expected to mourn the children of Iraq. People so trapped in an imagined America projected daily for profit by the media cannot possibly grasp how the massacre of innocent people thousands of miles away can be used to condition in them a reflexive nationalist spirit, fostering a vacant unity in the face of the profound degeneration of our republic.

To me, the most profound sort of moral blindness in heartland America is born of innocent trust in our system. The other day while loading groceries into my truck at the Food Lion parking lot, I ran into an old high school flame, Carolyn. At fifty-eight she is still at Rubbermaid, where she has worked for twenty years. Because of that she is still a trim, hard-body knockout with buns of steel and a country-girl smile that takes ten years off her face if it takes a day. It makes a blubbery old fat guy like me feel like crawling under my truck until she drives away. But I managed to say hello and make that sixty seconds of obligatory southern small talk. A "hi-bye" is not enough down here and is usually considered a snub. Noticing that Carolyn had four different kinds of "Support Our Troops" magnetic ribbons on her new Toyota, I said:

"Damn, Carolyn, couldn't you find space for another ribbon?"

"Actually," she sighed, "there was another one but somebody stole it—trying to make it look like they donated, I guess."

"Donated to what?"

"The money from the magnetic ribbons goes to support our troops," she replied.

"Who told you that?"

"Nobody. I just figure it does. Why else would they make 'em?"

I looked at her broad girlish-grown-older face and curly salt-and-pepper hair, and what I saw was not ignorance—though that too was there—but trust in some nonexistent system of the "way things ought to be." It's the sort of thing that makes college-educated people snicker when they encounter it but is honest and unencumbered by cynicism. The disconnect in this country can be so damned stunning sometimes that you don't know whether to laugh or cry, or what to say in the face of it.

"So how's Ron and the kids," I asked, with thirty seconds still to go.

In four hours Carolyn will walk through the doors of the concrete city of night and attach Rubbermaid safety gear onto that beautiful hard body. And she, like Tom and Nance, suspended in that crushing silence inside her noise-protection earmuffs, will never once ask herself why anybody has the right to make her pee into a bottle on demand, or whether the Democrats really do support the man-boy love crowd, or that most burning question of all, "Why do the Zen masters choose BRUTE?"

3

The Deep-Fried, Double-Wide Lifestyle

WHATEVER IT TAKES, THE MORTGAGE RACKET WILL PUT YOU UNDER YOUR OWN ROOF

PRINTED IN U.S.A.

Q: How does a redneck tell when the house trailer is level?
A: The snot runs out of both sides of the baby's nose at the same time.

"**I** can get a ham sandwich a home loan if the sandwich has a job," mortgage broker Mike Molden told me as he reared back in his $35 Wal-Mart desk chair in a space that resembled the recreation room of a 1940s bungalow. Clearly this office had recently been a residence, quickly converted into business space, and even then not completely. No pretense here. When I visited Mike in the spring of 2005, his company was among the thousands cranking out mortgages on folding tables to cash in on the housing boom—the one caused by the investment capitalists who came out of the dot-com bust of the late 1990s howling like scalded dogs and looking for another fat hog to cut. They found it in the mortgage industry, with a big thank-you to Alan Greenspan. By the time this book sees the stores, I am assuming it will be deader than Dallas on Monday night, or at least so "cooled down" you have to break the ice on a mortgage to sign it, but it's been a good ten-year ride.

Brokers like Mike are grateful for that ride. "Where else could a guy like me, with no education beyond high school, make $66,000 a year working only twelve hours a week?"

But Mike does not kid himself. He saved his money, knowing that, as author James Howard Kunstler put it: "The mortgage industry, a mutant monster organism of lapsed lending standards and arrant grift on the grand scale, is going to implode like a death star under the weight of these nonperforming loans and drag every tradable instrument known to man into the quantum vacuum of finance that it creates."

Not that the pumpkin-faced fifty-year-old fellow sitting in the plastic chair outside the broker's office door and waiting to apply for a loan grasps any of this. Tommy Ray drives a construction materials delivery truck and makes $9.50 an hour. He has had four jobs in two years. One was at the giant local milk processing complex, Hood Dairy, where people hold positions such as "missing children integration technician," meaning that you run a machine that slaps the pictures of missing children on milk cartons.

Mike Molden knows Tommy's kind well. Mike says, "He's got a buck fifty for a down payment. And he comes into my office, jams his fingers in his belt loops and says: 'Whatever it takes!'" Which to a mortgage broker translates as "Rape me." He will be accommodated.

Tommy Ray wants a loan to purchase a residential lot and a $79,000 "mobul hawm," the 2005 Riverine Forester model to be exact. The one with:

> Vaulted Ceiling with 7'6" sidewall height, Stipple textured ceilings, Glass light fixtures, Draperies, Carpeting w/ rebond carpet pad, Linoleum entry foyer, Wire and vent for dryer, Smoke detectors [*sic*]—all bedrooms, Flat panel oak cabinet doors, Dual control kitchen sink, 4" laminate backsplash, Cabinet above refrigerator, Range hood with light and vent. Fiberglass shower, towel bar and tissue holder, R-33 roof insulation . . .

Obviously, when the builders have to push the fact that the unit has towel bars and tissue holders and that the light fixtures are real glass, we are not talking the Hamptons. Still, if you can abandon all social pretense and class bigotry, or if you've ever lived in one, you know that house trailers do have their advantages. Millions of working folks were raised in them and see nothing wrong with a trailer lifestyle. It's easier than dealing with the average three-thousand-square-foot suburban home, and if you choose the right trailer park, you are surrounded by people similar to yourself, and people look out for one another's property without the need of a Neighborhood Watch. Frankly, the closer I get to sixty-five, the more attractive it looks to me— not that my wife, the lawn and garden queen, will ever go for it. But to me a trailer within walking distance of a nice creek or the ocean, with no lawn to mow and a good nearby beer joint where the geezers fart and lie up a storm . . . I could handle that. These are the kinds of reasons many working whites who can get a traditional home financed still choose a trailer.

A larger number, however, purchase trailers because it is the closest they will ever come to owning the place where they shit. And yes, they are quite aware that millions of more upscale people view them as white trash. ("Jeeter honey, pleeze don't piss off the front porch.")

America, as we are so often told, is a classless society. And without classes there can never be a class war (which does not prevent any politician who mentions class being accused of fomenting one). Well, I'm here to tell ya, honey, class hate between whites does exist. I'm eat up with the stuff! Case in point: Every time I see a local developer's bimbo wife sporting a fifty-dollar manicure and dropping her honky brat off at the $8,000-a-year Powhatan prep school down the road, I wanna rip her Martha Pink cashmere sweater off and stomp it. Every time I see some old-boy UVA lawyer posturing at the brew pub, I want to whup him upside the jaw with his authentic English ale glass. And I know I'm not alone in these feelings—I'm just willing to be honest about it. But for the most part, while the working woman who tracks freight on a computer screen in the K-mart warehouse may resent Mrs. Pink Cashmere, her dislike is unusually limited to giving her the finger when Mrs. Pink backs out in front of her in the mall parking lot. The truth is that she is afraid of Mrs. Pink. She has always been afraid of Mrs. Pink.

Back in high school, I once watched Rubbermaid Carolyn, who was working poor, broad-faced, and less attractive in those days, stifle tears and pretend to be unaffected when a doctor's daughter named Zemma mocked her for her rather ratty look. The doctor's daughter later married the guy who now runs the stock brokerage downtown, and they did so well during the 1990s that they recently made the newspaper for donating the equivalent of five years of my salary toward the restoration of our historic landmark high school, where he was a football star in his youth.

Carolyn married Ron. They just got their first new home in 2002—$273,000 with an adjustable rate mortgage, thanks to the credit bubble and a dodgy application nursed along by their mortgage broker. Carolyn never has to worry about bumping into Zemma again though, because Zemma lives out on Middle Road with the other moneyed folk, surrounded by their two-acre lawns fenced in the style of the landed gentry's horse farms.

Carolyn lives in Regency Lakes, a fancy name for a place behind the mall, where truck drivers park their big rigs in the driveways just like their daddies did and just like mine did when he "drove truck." Calling them poor would not be quite accurate, unless you used net worth as a gauge of prosperity. Then they would be worse than poor because poor is zero, and owing hundreds of thousands with no chance of ever paying it off is below the zero mark. But debt and poverty have no relationship in the American scheme of things, so let's just call Carolyn and Ron "poorish"—outwardly comfortable people who could be homeless next month.

What white middle America loathes these days are poor and poorish people, especially the kind who look and sound like they just might live in a house trailer. They will swear on a stack of Lands' End catalogs that they are not bigots, but, human nature being what it is, we are all kicking someone else's dog around, whether we admit it or not. The new terms of discrimination are all economic and about displays of true worth such as homes, vacations, and private education. Especially homes. And the most accurate measure of economic position is where you live and what you live in. It is here that wealth and status in society—or the lack—are displayed. Nothing says high-school- or junior-college-educated and earning in the midthirties like a $16,000 GM Sierra in front of a one-car-garage modular. Poorish with seven credit cards. And nothing says igner'nt and po' like a house trailer with a $39,000 dual-wheelie 350 HP GM classic version of the same damned GM Sierra parked in the drive.

There was a time when trailers did not carry the mark of the beast, when they were an important component of America's housing. The post–World War II years spawned the greatest housing shortage in our history, and that shortage was met with the house trailer—later rechristened the "mobile home," even though few of them ever moved once they were planted in a "trailer park." Sixty years later, most of those trailer parks are gone, many having been replaced with the plywood and plastic siding hell known as the modular home development. You've passed these homes being towed on the highway, the "modules" that look like a house sawed in half because that's exactly what they are.

The mobile home market is still thriving, and along with modular homes they are an integral part of American "White Trashonomics," and financing them is a lucrative business, which is where people like Mike Molden come in. I use the word *business* loosely. What I am talking about is a complex and nasty circle of credit racketeering by the mortgage and banking business based upon conditioned consumer stupidity and millions of very shaky credit applications. Apparently, anyone who refrains from discharging firearms in the broker's office and manages to make it to his or her job most mornings can get financing.

At any rate, Tommy Ray is standing in the broker's office with one of those shaky credit applications in his hand, and he has a plan. Judging from the credit application, it would appear that Tommy's plan is "quit your way to success." He quit his last job for the current one because it pays five cents an hour more. Honest to god, five cents. And he has to wait six months before he gets health insurance. Tommy explains it this way: "You gotta consider the overtime, which is seven cents an hour. They've promised me twenty hours overtime a week. See, that's my plan!" Which is how much? Fifteen bucks a week? Before taxes. Woo-hoo! He ultimately ended up having his hours cut below forty because he is delivering construction materials and it was a rainy spring and summer. That's the thing with white trashonomics: It never works out. But as Mike Molden tells me, "Everybody that comes in here has 'a plan.'"

As proof of established credit, Tommy has seven bright, glossy credit cards. All the worst offenders, like Capitol One and Providian—the ones that target high-risk clients and sport the highest interest rates, with total debt callable at any time and stunning penalties.

He thinks having so many is helping him build up credit, though naturally the lender will see them for what they are: seven opportunities to screw up. One of those cards comes courtesy of Gateway. Like most other clients here, Tommy has a computer. It's an ego thing. Gotta have one, even if he only uses it to get NASCAR results. Smokes, ammo, dog food, and a Dell—it's a lifestyle choice. Everyone has Dell or Gateway accounts on which the computer was purchased online, on credit at 30.54 percent interest. Many if not most of the Dell and Gateway accounts are in collection when the credit check is done for the loan. In fact, Mike tells me that these days you can have as much as twenty thousand dollars in collection at one time and still get a home loan. And you've been sweating your credit rating! It's all in the points you are willing to eat, a point being 1 percent of the loan amount.

The median credit rating in this country is allegedly 678, meaning one half of people are above that number and one half of people are below it. However, if the average person walking into Mike's office hits 600 it's a miracle. Credit scores in the working heartland often look like batting averages. But even at 500 you can get a 70 percent mortgage. Yet, realistically, who has, say, $65,000 lying around in the bank for a down payment on a $200,000 home? You are going to take those points right up the shorts and smile.

As we have said, the biggest organized racket in the United States rests upon the dream of owning one's own home. Hundreds of legally sanctioned scams operate under this ruse. Our economy depends upon continuous expansion of housing construction and financing of all types. The Federal Reserve tries to orchestrate the triangle of the United States, OPEC, and China. OPEC supplies oil, which allows the United States to build housing, which increases the money supply, which allows the United States to buy ever-cheaper manufactured junk from China and more oil from OPEC. The profits from this are dumped back into the United States, where they become more crackerbox-on-steroids McHousing at lower mortgage rates, enabling the cycle to be repeated. It goes something like that.

At the top end of the American shelter racket you have the new monster-bellum estates. At the very bottom are the people paying off the single-wide trailers sitting on rented space. The trailer is worth practically zilch the day it is sold and the owner has to pay for space to park it. This is the polar opposite of equity building. In fact, legally speaking, the mobile home owner is living in a vehicle and paying for a parking space, which is why trailers are titled like cars and have no deed. It says something about these working Americans that the absence of a deed to their home never strikes them as a drawback. "Title, deed—what's the difference?" says Tommy.

The next step up on the food chain is renting an apartment; the renter builds no equity but isn't locked into payments on a trailer that is losing value, and there's a certain freedom in being able to move without dragging along a worthless trailer. Next is the double-wide trailer attached to property; it is more livable and you own the property, which is presumably appreciating, or at least has some fluctuating but permanent value. Then comes the modular home attached to a lot, in which both the property *and* the housing may be appreciating until the modular home starts coming apart at the seams. And finally, there is the traditional "stick-built" home—the one that looks exactly like all its neighbors and suffers or flourishes along with the broader market. But there is a catch there, too: One-third of those homes are purchased with interest-only loans, which basically make the purchaser a renter, and therefore only nominally better off than the mobile home owner.

The high-pressure tactics used to sell all these except the traditional homes easily equal anything you will see at a used car dealership. We are talking pure lizard sleaze. With trailers and modular homes the buyer often signs the purchase and loan contracts before they have seen the home installed. Lenders distribute the loan funds to the dealer without an independent visual appraisal to ensure the home is worth enough to support the loan. Dealers falsify down payment information on credit applications, fake the terms and the price, and add on inflated fees from the word go. Most families start off owing far more than the home is worth. Dealers promise to pay off buyers' credit cards or other debts, adding nothing to the value of the home but jacking the loan skyward. So the buyer starts off "underwater" for the first fifteen years of payments. In about one-third of mobile home purchases even the down payment is borrowed, according to Consumers Union. When conventional home loans were running at 7 percent, trailer loans around Winchester were at 13 percent APR. More than half of all buyers finance points, and in some cases the points add as much as 5 percent to the loan.

Another mortgage broker friend, Rick Ostrander, reels me back in from my jeremiad against the mortgage industry. He says it operates by accepted American business practices, that it is no more predatory than any other type of business and is in some respects more honest: "To be fair, the mortgage business, for all its faults, is one in which the broker must disclose all the money he's making, in writing, and give the borrower a three-day right of rescission to walk away from the deal clean (no rescission period for purchases). Across the board, I don't see it as worse or more abusive than paying a 50 percent markup for a couch, or 500 percent for jewelry, or a flat-rate labor fee for car repair, not to mention buying a used car."

Another interpretation of "accepted American business practices" would be that scams are seen as an ordinary feature of the landscape. The fact remains that by the recommended standards of the National Consumer Law Center and the American Association of Retired Persons (AARP), more than three-quarters of mobile home loans could be considered predatory.

For the most part, the buyer doesn't get the chance to choose which predator. Once you are in the door of, let us say, Earl's Manufactured and Mobile Home Sales, old Earl is not going to let you get out the door to do any comparison shopping if he can help it. And he helps it quite a bit. Dealers discourage shopping around in a number of ways. For instance, although a credit check costs the dealer a few dollars at most, consumers are charged $25 or more for a credit check or an "application fee." I've heard of charges as high as $150. And usually there is another $300 to $400 deposit of some sort before you get away, just to keep you nailed down to that "attractive multisectioned manufactured home." The industry makes much noise about multisectioned manufactured homes and how nice they are these days, stressing that they are not trailers, but they are still plywood boxes shipped on wheels to the site just like house trailers.

Manufactured homes are always worth less than the principal outstanding balance on the loan contract. The buyer who tries to resell one during the early years of the loan will not be able to get a high enough price and will end up with a negative balance. And of course buyers with negative equity in their homes have less incentive to keep making payments when times get tough. Thus, many of them simply pack up and walk away. In the business it is called "relocating under cover of darkness."

Few of the people relocating under cover of darkness are *Beverly Hillbillies* types. They are ordinary working Americans, some of them making fair bucks. Take Karen and Marty. She is a physical therapist and Marty is a supervisor at the GE light bulb plant. They earn $42,000 and $40,000 respectively. According to the mortgage officer's calculations, they could comfortably afford a house costing $182,000. Nevertheless, comfort be damned, they came to him having chosen a house costing $320,000. So instead of the $1,500 a month mortgage they could afford, they ended up with a $2,700 interest-only mortgage. And why did they do that? Because the house was near a franchise burrito stand they liked! Which goes to show that a person can make good money and still have white trash sensibilities.

"The industry allows them to borrow to the absolute edge of their ability to repay," Mike says. "What we never see when we drive by those big developments are the people inside surviving on tuna fish sandwiches and living on the cusp of affordability. If gas and heating oil go up, they will lose their home. For example, it takes $250 a month for gas to commute and $300 a month for heating oil in winter. One bad winter or oil crisis and they are done for. I expect them to relocate under cover of darkness soon. It's only a matter of time," he says, until they walk away from that house and all the stuff they bought on credit to furnish it.

Measured by pure ownership of "stuff," working people have never been better off. Tom Henderson is cruising the boat shops for a new bass boat, and even Nance is considering a vacation in Cancún. None of them has any grasp of the staggering changes taking place in the world, least of all that they are living in a virtual reality that is utterly unsustainable. They are going to be steamed when the bottom falls out of the mortgage and construction games, when the cheap oil fiesta is over and even the Wal-Mart parking lot is empty.

The reality is that our economy now consists of driving 250 million vehicles around the suburbs and malls and eating fried chicken. We don't manufacture much. We just burn up everscarcer petroleum in the ever-expanding suburbs built with mortgage money lent to people who haven't a clue. Rick Ostrander writes me this morning: "With inventories of unsold homes now increasing and appreciation rates flattening or decreasing, plus all the other Peak Oil/global warming shit hitting, I think there we'll start to see major bankruptcies of lenders foundering with scads of unsellable housing stock on their books. And little tribes of squatters, gardeners, and salvage artists moving from vacant house to vacant house. The McMansion folks with their unheatable foyers and 5,000-square-foot master suites and 'too big to mow, too small to plow' yards are at least as dependent on two whomp-ass incomes as Joe Sixpack is on the wifey's part-time gig driving a school bus. It won't be too long before we're dismantling those McM's for their copper and firewood and gardening those three-acre 'estate' lots like coolies."

For towns like mine there is as much tragedy as folly in the superheated rip-and-run American housing boom. The engine of economic growth in Winchester and the surrounding county has been explosive suburban development. According to U.S. Census data, the Winchester/Frederick County statistical area is second in the state in percentage of new residential housing growth, and it ranks 152 out of 3,141 in the rate of "residential structure growth" among all U.S. counties. Counting all the road building, school construction, utilities, and other infrastructure, some $50 million to $100 million is injected annually into the area's economy, replacing wages lost due to outsourcing or simply because the jobs in question no longer fit into the new global economics. (There is not much demand for a shoe repairman in a world of cheap throwaway footwear, or much work for a radio repair shop when most people own plastic radios made in Taiwan.) Without the suburban development boom, our town would still be the sleepy county seat for a handful of redneck ass scratchers in the outer asteroid belt surrounding Washington, D.C. Directly or indirectly, the livelihood of everyone in Winchester—construction worker, banker, pizza boy, mortgage broker, and merchant and Mexican sod roller alike—is dependent upon expanding both the local and national sprawl of suburbs and office and low-wage "manufacturing campuses."

When the boom is over, when the creation of mortgages can no longer be sustained, there will be hell to pay. The national bankruptcy laws have just been revised to make a fresh start out of debt hard as hell, if not impossible. Meanwhile, the SUV or the Dodge Ram sits there in the garage gasping for more petrol and the heating bills nearly doubled last winter.

Having squandered all of our postwar wealth on construction of a vast nonsustainable suburban infrastructure, we are now trapped in a "psychology of previous investment," as James Howard Kunstler calls it. Letting go of the very thing that is sinking us is impossible for anyone like Tommy or Mike or Nance or Buck to imagine. How could we ever get loose of such an America: the cineplexes, outlet stores, trilevel overpasses, eight-thousand-square-foot "Tyvek houses," disposable double-wides, imported vitro ceramic gas ranges for the doctors' wives and Wal-Mart barbecues for guys like Pootie and me, Hummers and Hondas and Game Boys and Dale Earnhardt memorial crockpots and twelve-bucks-a-pair Chinese-made fake Birkenstocks, the big box stores and Olive Garden . . . the entire buzzing, blinking, digital phantasmagoria.

It has been an orgy so glorious and unholy, so mindless that we have now eaten our seed crop in our spiraling consumerism.

Our political masters look the other way. The Republicans have proclaimed the entire disastrous mess to be the lifestyle we are entitled to as Americans, and therefore nonnegotiable. The Democrats, even when they do have power, remain terrified of proposing any real change that would release us from our oil and sprawl addiction. To break free from our utter dependence upon thoughtless sprawl, we would have to end, just for starters, the reckless issuance of mortgages and the entire credit card business and invest in mass transit.

Global banking knows it. Top government officials know it. Most of the "developed world" understands it. And our White House leadership knows it, even as they, lost in pirate schemes for power, plunge toward the precipice, mad old men who've commandeered the nation as their getaway car, hoping to make an Evel Knievel jump over the canyon, hoping to get away clean with the whole shebang, the oil, the weapons contracts, everything . . . while from the backseat the silver spooners and the chickenhawk boys are yelling, "Fuck the oil slick, George, stomp it!"

The overfed and overspent throng, distracted by the national hologram, hasn't a clue. Working mooks like Tom Henderson and mortgage hustlers like Mike cling to the notion that everything is going to be okay. Yessiree, these things have a way of working out. Science will come up with an answer. Global warming will turn out to be like the Y2K scare, and we will go motoring off into the endless retail summer. These comforting assurances will be sustained by the corporate and political masters of the national hologram right up to the day our financial elites pack up their duds and head for their homes abroad. Contrary to popular belief, these homes are not usually located in storm-prone Caribbean islands alongside their secret tax-free bank accounts, which according to the *Christian Science Monitor* hold more than $11.5 trillion—an amount greater than the U.S. national debt and equal to a third of the world's assets. The richest four hundred Americans alone have $1.2 trillion in assets, with the rest distributed among 793 wealthy and powerful people. Of course, when the deal does go down, all hell is going to break loose in this country. But for now we live in that eerie space purchased through sheer denial. That horrible fetid calm before the storm.

Incidentally, Tommy Ray got the loan for his $79,000 trailer, which somehow added up to $130,000 in total. The lot to put it on, a specially required septic tank, a driveway, power, and so on set him back another $50,000. His $130,000 investment will be worth a little more than half of what he paid for it the day after he signs the contract, and it will cost him $260,000 before it is paid off.

So is he just a sucker with no common sense at all? Not really. Tommy is a guy with two grown kids and a wife who works in food service at the hospital for $6 an hour and thinks this would be the most beautiful place she has ever lived. And she is right. And big-hearted Tommy is happy to see her happy. Tommy also has a crippled dog, born without hind legs. He didn't have the heart to put it to sleep, so now that dog drags himself around on the carpet basking in their affection and care. Any place they live is a real home that smells like popcorn and fresh laundry and home cooking and has more humanity than any McMansion I've ever been in.

Still, Tommy is a guy who often cannot get forty hours' work at a living wage and has to scramble for a nickel more an hour, then kid himself that opportunity is knocking at his door. I know these things because he's a relative of mine. And like many others in my family, he was taught by his experience in American society that he is not worthy of a traditional house or decent treatment in the labor market or a living wage. The relentless, autocratic blue-collar American workplace has ground these people down, rendered them unable to imagine the kind of self-determination their World War II–era daddies had. Like so many Americans, their concept of personal freedom has now been reduced to a pale facsimile—to the symbolism of gun ownership or the freedom to express their individuality by buying and squirreling away more meaningless junk. More is better and bigger is best but brand new and big as a house is best of all. So this 2005 Riverine Forester trailer with the 2-by-2-inch interior wall studs and flat-panel oak cabinet doors looks to Tommy like destiny. And when you encounter destiny, you stick your fingers in your belt loops and say, "Whatever it takes, man. Whatever it takes."

4

Valley of the Gun

BLACK POWDER AND BUCKSKIN IN HEARTLAND
AMERICA

"Take 'em, Joe!" cried Grandpap as the three deer, a buck and two does, stretched out at a lope across the ridgeline above us, swift dark silhouettes against the tan buckwheat stubble of what we called the ridgefield. My father, "Big Joe," leaned into the frost-tinged air. KA-KRAK, KA-KRAK, KA-KRAK, KA-KRAK—the sound of each shot was followed by that rattling echo through the chilled gray woods that every meat hunter knows and can hear in his sleep. The first deer, the buck, was thrown sideways by the impact and went down at a running roll. The two does did approximately the same thing; the second one would later be found after an hour of tracking the blood on fences and grass. We had just witnessed an amazing feat still talked about in the Bageant family all these years after my father's death.

That was in the late fall of 1957. I had been allowed to go with the deer hunters for the first time, and already I had seen family history made. Dad had stepped into family folklore, become one of those to be talked about for generations in a family of hunters, mentioned in the same breath with old Jim Bageant, who shot a whole washtub full of squirrels one November morning just before World War II.

These men—Daddy, Grandpap, and two of my uncles, Uncle Toad and Uncle Nelson—were meat hunters who trudged the fields and woods together right up until the day they got too crippled up to do it or died. And it was because they were meat hunters that they let my dad take the three deer, one each on their tags, on the last legal day of hunting season. Everyone knew that my dad, the best shot in the family, had the most likelihood of getting more than one of the deer.

Later in the day, after dressing the deer and hanging them on the back porch to chill, we sat around the living-room woodstove, cleaned the guns, and talked about the day's hunt. To an eleven-year-old boy, the smell of gun oil and the stove's searing raw heat on the face, the polishing of blued steel and walnut, the clean raspy feel of the checked gun grips, the warm laughter of the men, well . . . that's primal after-the-hunt stuff so deep you can feel the sparks from Celtic yew log fires and the brush of bearskin leggings on your knees. It has been going on in this place and on this land for 250 years.

I quit hunting years ago, yet this remembered room and the long-dead men who inhabited it that day in the fall of '57 remain for me one of the truest and finest places and events on this earth. Guns can have a place inside a man, even remembered guns in the soul of an arthritic sixty-year-old old socialist writer. The crack of a distant rifle or the wild meat smell of a deer hanging under a porch lightbulb on a snowy night still bewitches me with the same mountain-folk animism it did when I was a boy. And though I have not hunted since 1986, the sight of a fine old shotgun still rouses my heart.

In families like mine, men are born smelling of gun oil amid a forest of firearms. The family home, a huge old clapboard farmhouse, was stuffed with guns, maybe thirty in all. There were 10-, 12-, 14-, and 20-gauge shotguns, pump guns, over-and-unders, and deer rifles of every imaginable sort from classic Winchester 94 models to 30-ought-sixes, an old cap and ball "horse pistol" dating back to the mid-1800s, and even a set of dueling pistols that had been in my family since the 1700s. No hillbilly ever threw a gun away, even when it could no longer be repaired. And until they stopped working completely, guns were endlessly cared for and patched back together. Otherwise they weren't to be parted with except under the direst circumstances, either on your deathbed or because you were so broke your cash bounced. For example, there is one ancestral family gun that my brother Mike did not inherit—my father's prized old Ivers and Johnson double-barrel shotgun, which had been in the family since the turn of the twentieth century. An out-of-work trucker at Christmastime, Daddy sold it to buy us kids the standard assortment of Christmas junk so we would not feel disappointed. I remember a Robert the Robot for me, a tin stove for my sister, a little red wheelbarrow for my brother, and, of course, toy guns and holsters. That was in 1952. We still have the photographs, and we still lament the loss of that fine old Ivers and Johnson.

Through our early years we boys could not hunt, but we were allowed to beat rabbits out of the bush for the dogs to chase back around to the hunters. With clothes torn in the blackberry thickets and feet frozen in the winter creeks, faces pricked and bleeding, we rustled the brush piles. This would be considered child abuse today, but so would a lot of things we once did. Besides, there are far fewer boys hunting nowadays, thanks to computer games and television. Anyway, surviving the brush torture test of manhood earned us the right to sit around with the menfolk when they told hunting stories—so long as we kept our mouths shut unless spoken to. It was then we learned the family lore, who did what back when and with which gun. This imbued each gun with a sense of ancestry, made us feel part of a long and unbroken chain of men, a history we would contemplate over decades of seasons during that long patient waiting game that makes up most of successful hunting—or getting skunked.

After a couple more years came a day when they let us help clean the guns, running oil-soaked patches down the barrels and polishing the stocks and metalwork self-consciously under the eyes of grandfathers, fathers, and uncles, our mouths set serious and every move as careful as if each gun were made of dynamite, trying to demonstrate that we respected their destructive capability enough to be trusted with one. Then the mighty time came when Pap would pull the small 22-caliber "cat rifle" down from the bedroom wall to begin real target practice, along with what would today be called gun-safety training, though it was more instinct and common sense for farm boys back then. We had observed gun-carrying practices for years, absorbing such lessons as these: Never crawl through a fence with a loaded gun. Never point a gun at anyone, even accidentally while walking together. Never kill anything you are not going to eat, unless it is a varmint like a groundhog or a pest such as a copperhead snake under the front porch. Never shoot in the known direction of a house, no matter how distant. In 251 years of hunting these hills, no one in the Bageant clan was ever accidentally shot while hunting, which testifies to the practical responsibility native to the three-century-old gun culture of the southern uplands.

Half a dozen years after the Christmas Daddy sold the Ivers and Johnson, I turned thirteen, grown up enough to start hunting with an old family 12-gauge, the entire barrel and forestock of which was held together with black fabric "tar tape," as electrical tape was then called. And when I looked down at that 12-gauge shotgun cradled in my arm under a bright cold October sky, I knew that my grandfather had walked the same fields with it when it was brand-new from the Sears catalog, and had delivered mountains of meat to the smoky old farmhouse kitchen with it. I knew that my father had contemplated all this too under the same kind of sky, carrying the same gun, and that my younger brother would too. Ritual and clan. My family has hog-butchering knives that have been passed along for generations. I've heard that Norwegian carpenters do the same with tools. And perhaps there is the same ritual passing of male family heritage and custom when upper-class sons of, say, the Bush family go off to the alma mater prep school and are handed the keys to the Lincoln. I wouldn't know. My symbol of passage was an old shotgun with black tape along the barrel.

For millions of families in my class, the first question asked after the death of a father is "Who gets Daddy's guns?" That sounds strange only if you did not grow up in a deeply rooted hunting culture. My brother Mike uses the same guns our daddy used. If there is a hunting gene, he's got it, so he inherited the family guns. True to form, Mike is a meat hunter who puts a couple of bucks and a doe in the freezer every year and probably could bring them home given only a bag of rocks with which to hunt.

If you were raised up hunting, you know that it is a ritual of death and plenitude, an animistic rite wherein a man blows the living heart out of one of God's creatures and then, if he deserves to be called a hunter, feels deep, honest gratitude for the creator's bounty. The meat on our tables links us to the days of black powder and buckskin. I can see why millions of urban citizens whose families came from teeming European cities through Ellis Island don't understand the links between Celtic and Germanic settler roots, guns, survival, and patriotism. Gunpowder is scarcely a part of their lives. Unfortunately, utter lack of knowledge and experience doesn't keep nonhunting urban liberals from believing they know what's best for everybody else—or simply laughing at what they do not understand.

To nonhunters, the image conjured by the title of this book might seem absurd, rather like a NUKE THE WHALES bumper sticker. But the title also captures something that moves me about the people I grew up with—the intersection between hunting and religion in their lives. The link between protestant fundamentalism and deer hunting goes back to colonial times, when the restless Presbyterian Scots, along with English and German Protestant reformers, pushed across America, developing the unique hunting and farming-based frontier cultures that sustained them over most of America's history. Two hundred years later, they have settled down, but they have not quit hunting and they have not quit praying. Consequently, today we find organizations such as the Christian Deer Hunters Association (christian deerhunters.org), which offers convenient pocket-size books of meditations, such as *Devotions for Deer Hunters*, to help occupy the time during those long waits for game. Like their ancestors, deer hunters today understand how standing quietly and alone in the natural world leads to contemplation of God's gifts to man. And so, when a book like *Meditations for the Deer Stand* is seen in historical context, it is no joke. For those fortunate enough to spend whole days quietly standing in the November woods just watching the Creator's world, there is no irony at all in the notion that his son might be watching too, and maybe even willing to summon a couple of nice fat does within shooting range.

Something about the smell of black-powder smoke and portojohn chemicals stirs patriotic feelings in the hearts of certain Americans, making them want to camp in the rain so they can spend days along a firing line and blasting away at clay flower pots and sailing skeet with shot and ball. Consequently, I am peering from under a poncho in the October drizzle watching some forty-five hundred mostly working-class Americans blazing away with rifles, muskets, cannons, and even Civil War mortars. Welcome to Fort Shenandoah, located on several hundred acres of woods and hills along Back Creek in Frederick County, Virginia. Operated by the North-South Skirmish Association, it is dedicated to the ignition of black powder in all its forms, and to black-powder competition in musket, carbine, smoothbore, breechloader, revolver, mortar, and artillery, not to mention the junior BB-gun division.

On this particular day I am trudging through the fog and wood smoke past the cabins and RV camps of dozens of reactivated Civil War units with names such as the 27th North Carolina, the

Cockade Rifles, the 2nd Regiment Virginia Volunteers, the 7th West Virginia Volunteer Infantry, and the Richmond Cavalry. On my left across the creek bed for hundreds of yards stretches the firing line. The thick grumble and crackle of a thousand muskets going off gives some idea of what a battle must have been like as the streaks of orange fire snap out through the mist and drizzle. Most of the people gathered here are reenactors, but not all. Some of the best shooters are black-powder enthusiasts and amateur gunsmiths. Some wear authentic uniforms, most of them in sizes far larger than any Civil War soldier ever wore, owing to modern American corpulence. Some are traditional blue-collar workers, but there are also optometrists, schoolteachers, and the occasional attorney, professor, or physician.

It's a thought-provoking experience wherein one is struck by the violence of so much of American history. One is also moved by the ordinary decency of the folks honoring an idealized, schoolbook-simple American heritage here today. These are some of the most sincere people America has to offer: hardworking men who do not cuss or drink in front of the kids and are spending a long weekend with their wives and children. Every one of them owns at least one gun, and most own several. Most would die for or kill for America as they understand it.

Which is a damned shame because the way they understand it is through the purposefully clouded lens of the Fox News Network and the jingoistic history they learned in school. Few honestly grasp that there are other nations in the world, other value systems. True, some have been abroad, but generally within the controlled environment of the military. Others who have traveled to Europe for pleasure experienced it the same as most

Americans regardless of class or income—as a destination theme park existing solely for their amusement. The majority of working-class Americans, including those on this firing line at Fort Shenandoah, have always been an "ain't been nowhere and don't care to go" kind of people. Urban and suburban sophisticates snicker at the kitschiness of an overweight father and son shooting team being served beans around a campfire by Mom wearing calico. Somehow, swim meets and biking along concrete paths in the suburbs and cities are supposed to be superior family activities.

Walking through Fort Shenandoah's wet woods excavates memories. I hunted rabbits out here as a kid and courted a little gal up the road at the tiny village of Gainesboro. She was the first in a short string of women (three) who've suffered the indignities of being married to me. There was a time not so long ago when this location was remote both geographically and culturally. People who lived here in the 1930s remember going down to the road—"Old 600" it is called—on Saturday night to throw rocks at passing cars and strangers, hoping some passing motorist would jump out to fight with them. George Washington once commented that some backwoods people here darted from tree to tree, peeping out and giggling when he rode by. Pleasing as it is to believe our colonial frontier settlers were all noble Dan'l Boones, I suspect the socially isolated, darkly ignorant, and, yes, violent folks Washington talked about were far more common.

That dark strain is still to be found here along Back Creek and Hogue Creek running behind Gainesboro. Even when I was a kid in the fifties and sixties, it was dangerous on weekends in Gainesboro. The infamous Kane brothers, the Halidays, and the

Branson boys (not their real names) happily beat the living hell out of anyone they encountered. Period. For no reason whatsoever. Just drunk. It was anger born of ignorance and Scots-Irish acculturation. It was also about our perception of being lower class and of lacking any imaginable future. We were one step above the blacks and several steps below just about anybody from "the city." Even being from "in town," as Winchester was then and is now referred to by county natives, was a definite health risk out here on weekends.

Returning to these woods and fields, where many of the oldest families still live much as always on their farms (though with the accoutrements of modern life, such as satellite dishes mounted into 259-year-old brick), is comforting because of the smell of wood smoke and the way the fingers of fog creep ghostlike around woodpiles, decaying barns, and the occasional corn-crib and old stone well house deep in the blackberry thickets. But just a few ridges away are the people coming and going to the shopping centers and commuting into Washington, D.C., who've forced the sale of most of these old places. The owners of these ancient farms can no longer afford the taxes on two hundred acres that the rest of the world sees as better used for housing. And their children, as often as not among the commuters, are more than glad to accept a national developer's cash offer.

Somewhere in between are the rest of us natives, in whom such change revives long-buried anger at those faraway people who seem to govern the world: city people, educated city people who win and control while the rest of us work and lose. Snort at the proposition if you want, but that was the view I grew up with, and it still is quite prevalent, though not so open as in those days. These are the sentiments the fearful rich and the Republicans capitalize on in order to kick liberal asses in elections.

The Democrats' 2006 midterm gains should not fool anyone into thinking that these feelings are not still out here in this heartland that has so rapidly become suburbanized. It is still politically profitable to cast matters as a battle between the slick people, liberals all, and the regular Joes, people who *like* white bread and Hamburger Helper and "normal" beer. When you are looking around you in the big cities at all those people, it's hard to understand that there are just as many out here who never will taste sushi or, in all likelihood, fly on an airplane other than when we are flown to boot camp, compliments of Uncle Sam. Only 20 percent of Americans have ever owned a passport. To the working people I grew up with, sophistication of any and all types, and especially urbanity, is suspect. Hell, those city people have never even fired a gun. Then again, who would ever trust Jerry Seinfeld or Dennis Kucinich or Hillary Clinton with a gun? At least Dick Cheney hunts, even if he ain't safe to hunt with. George W. Bush probably knows a good goose gun when he sees one. Guns are everyday tools, like Skil saws and barbecue grills.

So when the left began to demonize gun owners in the 1960s, they not only were arrogant and insulting because they associated all gun owners with criminals but also were politically stupid. It made perfect sense to middle America that the gun control movement was centered in large urban areas, the home to everything against which middle America tries to protect itself—gangbangers, queer bars, dope-fiend burglars, swarthy people jabbering in strange languages. From the perspective of small and medium-size towns all over the country, antigun activists are an overwrought bunch.

Sooner or later, however, antigun hysteria touches even the smallest heartland burgs. Take the case of seventeen-year-old Joshua Phelps of Pine Bush, New York, population 1,539. Pine Bush resembles any small town in Virginia. Its dominant ethnic group (by a small margin) is Scots Irish—its roots hinted at by the fact that it is located in Orange County (named for William of Orange) next to Ulster County. In Pine Bush the median value of a new house even before the market downturn was $239,000, about the same as in Virginia, and ERA realtors unabashedly proclaim the "median house value *above* state average" and the "black race population percentage *significantly below* state average" (emphasis theirs, not mine). In race-sensitive Virginia, where elections are still being monitored under the 1965 Voting Rights Act for racial discrimination—as are elections in Brooklyn, Queens, and the Bronx, by the way—no realtor would have the balls to openly make such a statement, oft whispered though it be.

In October 2004 Joshua Phelps was a senior at Pine Bush High School and a member of the high school's Civil War Club. One day, after participating in a local reenactment of the Battle of Chancellorsville, he threw his Yankee uniform and blank-firing replica musket into his vehicle. Later, a school security guard spotted the musket and called the cops. Phelps was pulled from study hall, handcuffed by the police, and charged with criminal possession.

Josh, an enthusiastic B student, had joined the Civil War Club through school recruitment. Like many kids these days, he was trying to expand his extracurricular activities to beef up his college applications with the least effort and most fun. The school had issued him the blank-firing replica musket. In New York State bringing a replica gun onto school grounds is not a crime. None of this mattered. Josh was charged as if he'd had an AK-47 assault rifle or a rocket-propelled grenade in his vehicle, and he was kicked out of school. The school board defended its right to have him arrested, and, given the board's position, the police chief refused to drop the charges.

Then came the usual hairsplitting over what is and is not a gun. The legal eagles argued that Joshua could have stuffed the replica musket with gunpowder and a lead ball and used his underpowered one-shot wonder to kill half the student body. And so, in a mostly Republican, gun-owning, hunting town situated near the Pine Bush hunting and fishing preserve, an embarrassed seventeen-year-old was hauled into court and charged with criminal possession of a firearm. Ultimately, in a fit of common sense unusual in these frenzies, the judge suspended the charges. But the incident remains a topic of conversation in Pine Bush and will be cited around supper tables for years to come as an example of antigun histrionics, damaging liberal credibility on the subject of guns.

When I was seventeen, if I had left a gun in the car unattended on the school grounds, nothing would have happened. Like some other rural folks of my generation around here, I attended schools where boys kept 22-caliber rifles in their lockers to hunt groundhogs after school. And if the school principal had had any objections, he simply would have called my daddy, who would have kicked my ass, grounded me for a month, and made me clean the grease pit at the gas station/garage where he worked.

Before I am reminded that this is not 1960, let me describe the difference in the times. In 1960 common sense was equally distributed between liberals and conservatives. In those days, even liberal personages such as Democratic senator and vice president Hubert Humphrey said repeatedly that guns had a place in the home because history has shown that governments, even the best of them, have a habit of oppressing people who cannot defend themselves at their own front doors. Imagine any Democrat saying that aloud today.

Across rural and small-town America any kind of gun control is seen as an attempt to take away citizens' rights to protect home and hearth from the crazies and, increasingly, from an authoritarian government. Most of the people at Fort Shenandoah see gun ownership in this light—as a way of stopping the jackboots at their own front doors. Given what we've seen lately, I'm not so sure I don't agree with them. Of all the issues—gay marriage, abortion, affirmative action, animal rights—that have split American liberalism up into the honking gaggle of issue and identity cults it has become, gun ownership is the one that touches the lives of the most heartland voters. It reaches nearly everyone, even those who do not own guns. The right to do so rings liberty bells for them.

And why not? With Michael Savage and Ann Coulter openly calling for putting liberals in concentration camps, with the CIA now licensed to secretly detain American citizens indefinitely, and with the current administration effectively legalizing torture, the proper question to ask an NRA member these days may be, "What kind of assault rifle do you think I can get for three hundred bucks, and how many rounds of ammo does it take to stop a two-hundred-pound born-again Homeland Security zombie from putting me in a camp?" Which would you prefer, 40 million gun-owning Americans on your side or theirs?

Sure, kids have found their parents' guns and accidentally shot their little sisters, though damned few, as we shall presently see. And yes, there are too many guns in the wrong hands on the street. But until we find the guts to reverse the corporate purchase of our political system, the gun-industry-owned NRA leadership (the actual membership is not made up of armed nut cases as liberal pundits proclaim) and the gun industry are going to own the politicians and keep bearbaiting gun owners with the uninformed antics of the left and gun control groups.

Despite all I have said about how guns can have a deeper meaning and symbolism for Americans, including myself, I must tell you that I don't own or keep guns in my house these days. I am more attached to the warm memory of their place in my family heritage than I am to owning one. But more than 70 million responsible taxpaying Americans do own and enjoy more than 200 million guns. Doesn't it seem more reasonable to take action to heal the social pathology that generates crime than to use gun control to blow another political toe off American liberalism during each election cycle?

During this visit to Fort Shenandoah I stop by a New York Cavalry cabin at the edge of the creek. Inside, at a greasy plank table, Ed Cleary squints, sucks in on a Kool cigarette, and sticks the insulin hypodermic into his bony white thigh. His buddy Charlie Ross, wearing boxer shorts and flip-flops, is frying up some eggs on the stove. Charlie insists that I eat with them at the table, over which is a large smoke-stained banner, deep red with a picture of Lincoln and a New York Cavalry emblem in gold and blue. Ed and Charlie are down from Buffalo, New York, to shoot in the national musket competition, poke at the stove's innards, and maybe drink a little too much beer for their health without the women around. Ed joined the cavalry unit of reenactors who built this cabin before he retired from the Buffalo police force in 1996. Now he is free to bang around with his pal Charlie as they see fit, even if it means frying eggs and scratching your big white belly as you please and putting cigarettes out on the floor.

Standing up from the plank table, Ed opens the wood stove, and flicks the spent hypodermic into the fire. Charlie declares the eggs to be as ready as they'll ever be. So we sit down to eat and talk. "The people here at the fort," Charlie explains, "are not necessarily reenactors, despite their uniforms. They are 'enthusiasts.' As for us, there ain't much demand for seventy-year-old Civil War soldiers, but we still come down here to burn a little meat and black powder twice a year. You don't have to be able to charge up a hill to compete in the shooting events." Almost as if to prove his point, a very fat man with one leg amputated, wearing a Confederate uniform, rides by the door on a Rascal scooter.

Turns out that Charlie has just purchased a replica 1864 Spenser carbine at a nearby gun show. This brings up a discussion of Virginia's reputation as the "gun-running capital of the nation." Representatives from Washington, D.C., and urban areas such as Richmond have insisted that Virginia begin requiring instant background checks for firearm purchases at shows. Virginia's senate, however, has consistently blocked efforts to "close the loophole" in gun control law allowing people to buy firearms from unlicensed vendors such as collectors and private sellers at gun shows without on-the-spot criminal-background checks. For one thing, such background checks are hard for a small-time collector to set up. Gun control advocates argue that this loophole permits criminals to acquire weapons. And it probably does to some degree.

Charlie snorts in reply: "Ever been to a collector's gun show? Ever see the kind of people who attend? You don't find the meth-heads and the gangbangers at the gun shows. Believe me. They wouldn't be very comfortable. Ya gotta give the gun show sellers and collectors a little credit, for Christ's sake. They ain't stupid, and they don't want to see criminals carry guns any more than you do. And they get sick of people underestimating and bad-mouthing them. There's supposed to be hundreds of crimes committed with guns bought at gun shows in Virginia. I just don't believe it."

Ed the ex-cop does not completely agree, but as a guy who has slammed more criminals in the hoosegow than he can remember, he has some blunt ideas about the crime behind city-dwelling liberals' fear of anything resembling a gun. "There's a solution to most of it. It's the thing nobody's gonna do because it's too late and maybe can't be done now anyway. Get the dope off the streets. Do that and you'll whack the crime rate. But all this hysterical 'crime is caused by guns' shit doesn't cut it, I'm telling you. A hard-core crack head will just as soon rob you with a hammer or a knife. You gotta go after the real problem. Dope."

"Well goddam Sherlock Holmes!" observes Charlie.

And don't even get Ed going on the subject of guns and kids. He calls it "the most ass-hat Hollywood liberal New York Jew cause of all, except maybe protecting pornographers." Which works out great for me because I happen to have in my satchel material regarding Hollywood's obsession with gun violence and its effect on kids (two things Hollywood never dreamed of exploiting for profit, mind you). To wit, Handgun Control Inc. (HCI) is an organization dedicated to gun control for public safety. In an "Open Letter to the National Rifle Association," HCI proclaims in high dudgeon: "We hate what guns are doing to our communities, our schools, our families and, most especially, our children." Signing this open letter were numerous Hollywood figures ("all the regular Chardonnay suckers," as Ed calls them): Baldwin, Bergen, Brinkley, Cher, Donahue, De-Generes, Gere, Geraldo, Madonna, Nicholson, O'Donnell, Pfeiffer, Sarandon, Streep, Streisand, and Springsteen.

Personally, I love 'em all, but Hollywood doesn't seem to have the common sense God gave a soggy animal cracker when it comes to guns. Maybe they signed up to endorse HCI because their agent says they need a cause and there is no more room on the AIDS bandwagon. I don't know. But according to HCI and the well-meaning but clueless stars who endorse it, "Every day we lose thirteen children to gun violence in this country. . . . This debate is not about guns. It's about children." Nah. It's about middle-class liberal feel-good masturbation and celebrity-identity franchise building through causes. In reality, 90 percent of the "children" we lose to gun violence are gangbangers between fifteen and nineteen years of age. Which is not quite the same as your average elementary or middle school kid shooting up the neighborhood or popping little brother with daddy's Magnum pistol.

Even allowing for Columbine, the truth is that Americans, urban Americans included, have an excellent record when it comes to keeping guns out of the hands of kids. Accidental gun deaths among children are rare and by no means the epidemic HCI decries. Consider New York City—that great monument in the mid-American mind to metrosexuality, murder, and mayhem. The city has more than 2.6 million children under the age of ten, yet accidental gun deaths in that age group average only 1.2 per year, even with some 3.5 million guns owned by adults. Common sense tells us that most people, New Yawkers included, are very careful with their firearms. Like Ed, I have become deaf to the righteous wailing of the antigun intelligentsia in the brownstones of Chelsea, most of whom would strap on a Glock pistol if lox and corned beef ran wild in Central Park.

"Democrats need to get a grip," says Ed, sopping a piece of bread in his egg yolk, "maybe think for themselves for a change instead of getting all their ideas from NPR." Incidentally, Ed was a Democrat for the first fifty years of his life; he became a Republican shortly before Bush's election. He told me why: "I just reached the point where I looked at the Democratic Party and said, 'Enough is enough.' It had nothing to do with guns or gun control, though the way Democrats dealt with that issue was typical of everything they do these days. They act like there're no such things as values. Without values life just gets cheaper by the day because we no longer value anyone else's interests but our own. Meanwhile every twisted goat fucker with a bomb and a hundred bucks can buy a passport and a ticket to the U.S. while the Democrats are wringing their hands about diversity and writing more gun laws."

I point out that there are more than twenty thousand state, federal, and municipal gun laws, including thousands of local ordinances. If, like the Brookings Institution, you narrow it down to major federal laws and unique state laws, there are three hundred. Either way, they abound.

"Hell, yes," says Ed. "If gun laws were the answer, we'd have zero gun crimes. Right? Ain't a cop in the country believes gun laws are the answer. And even the judges are carrying Glocks."

"Judges? You kid me, Eddie boy," I said, feigning disbelief even though I'd stumbled on this information earlier.

"No. Really. You got any idea how many judges carry a gun? At least half of 'em."

Nowhere near half of judges carry arms in most states, but Ed is not completely off base. The U.S. Marshals Service does not track how many judges, sitting federal and state judicial officers, magistrates, or bankruptcy judges pack heat inside courtrooms. But estimates in law newsletters run as high as 25 percent or more in gun-friendly states such as Texas and Oklahoma, and in the single digits in some New England states. There are enough of them that the U.S. Judicial Conference, an organization representing the nation's federal bench, asked Congress to set federal judges free from local and state gun laws. The resulting proposed legislation—HR 1752—is broadly enough worded to allow a judge to carry a shotgun into the courthouse. At this writing, some senators think maybe a clause requiring gun-safety training for judges might be a good idea. Ed, however, seems to have no qualms about shotgun judges.

"Ya fucking straight. Can you see the look in the perp's eyes when Judge Roy Bean walks in with a Magnum 12-gauge?"

"Can you see the look in the antigun lawyer's eyes when he notices that Glock strapped to the judge's ankle?" I add.

"Good luck to the antigun nuts," replies Ed.

"I'll drink to that," I said.

"Not until at least noon you won't," Ed laughs.

Meanwhile, I am left to consider that most rednecks I know do not even bother to own a handgun—"pussy pistol" in the local vernacular. If you think you may need to kill somebody for whatever reason, wimpy handguns that barely produce a flesh wound are for cab drivers. A good 12-gauge pump-action shotgun loaded with double-ought buckshot will blow a hole in a man big enough to kick a football through.

Plenty of other cherished notions about guns are also the purest-grade horseshit. Take the laws against "plastic" guns. Remember them—the "terrorist specials"? There never was any such thing, but even the National Rifle Association supported this legislation, which provided fake cures for fake threats. Allegedly, plastic frames and grips made these guns invisible to metal detectors. Forget that no one ever made a workable gun without a metal or a metal-lined barrel, and forget that in "plastic" Glocks there is over a pound of metal, enough to send any airport detector into shrieking fits. Nothing to do but pass a law, so Senator Strom Thurmond (R—S.C.) and Senator Howard Metzenbaum (D—Ohio)—strange bedfellows—introduced a bill setting the minimum metal requirement at 3.2 ounces, less than a fifth of the metal contained in the "plastic" Glocks. The bill passed in a rare act of bipartisanship on Capitol Hill. No gun maker lost a nickel, and the politicians came off appearing concerned.

Maybe the biggest snow job was the campaign against "cop-killer" bullets. These bullets were invented to pierce the bullet-proof vests of criminals or the materials behind which criminals may be hiding. Made of tungsten, they were sold only to police and were not available in stores. As Ed says, "The cops never used these bullets, much less the criminals. Ordinary rifle ammo will penetrate a bulletproof vest at the right range. Cops never used them because they passed cleanly through the criminal without much wounding him. Cops would rather use a hollow point that spreads out and blows a real hole in the sumnabitch. Right? The manufacturers still sell the cop-killer bullets to police departments that still do not use them."

Any politician who exposes this kind of legislation for what it is gets scalded like a chicken-killing dog by the left and called a whore of the NRA. But to the millions of Americans who understand guns and how they work, that politician looks like an informed man telling the truth. Without a doubt the left would do much better if it stopped yammering about guns and redirected that energy toward fair wages or health care.

"That would be the smart thing," says Ed, "but not the liberal thing."

"The left just doesn't get it sometimes," I concede.

Then Ed says, "Hey, check out the side window!"

All I can see is Boy Scout Troop 107 conducting its annual popcorn and firewood sale. "No, I mean over there at the Alabama Raccoon Rough's campfire," Ed says.

Yup. It's a sight to warm three old guys' hearts—a voluptuous fifty-year-old babe with a Confederate flag on the seat of her jeans pouring coffee for the men assembled there.

"What's not to like about that, fellas?"

Not a damned thing, Ed. Not one damned thing.

Recalling Ed and Charlie in their funky old guys' lair by the creek, it occurs to me that not once did we mention the Second Amendment. But then not many ordinary citizen gun owners discuss the Second Amendment much, except for the online crowd. They either take the right for granted, as most Americans, gun owning and non–gun owning, have done throughout history, or they share the general sentiment of people in places like Fort Shenandoah: "Try and stop me." Whatever one's opinion of the folks at Fort Shenandoah, they are exercising their Second Amendment rights. And they will retain those rights.

Politicians understand this, even if the antigun portion of the public does not. Nearly twice as many people own guns as vote in this country—41 million voters versus 70 million gun owners. According to GAO fact sheets and other research, approximately half of American households have one or more guns. Some are for sport but more are for personal protection.

Every new attempt at gun control kickstarts thousands of additional purchases. You might think our Second Amendment right to bear arms would be one of the most commonly defended rights, given its popularity. Yet the Second Amendment remains the orphan of constitutional rights. The civil rights and civil liberties groups best suited and equipped to defend it would rather drink lye than publicly stand up for the Second Amendment. And that's a shame because conservative defense of the Second Amendment has been mostly a series of political stunts that make a mockery of a right older than the Republic itself, with deep roots in English political thought. American political historians too have consistently written off as unimportant the Second Amendment, whose rights are deeply grounded in the English Bill of Rights—progenitor of our own right to bear arms and written during a period of great civil unrest in England. Many have interpreted the Second Amendment as being about hunting rights. The Supreme Court, fond as it is of citing Blackstone's *Commentaries,* interprets Blackstone to suit its own prevailing mix of judges and the times when it comes to the Second Amendment. What the hell do the tea-slurping Brits know about guns?

Constitutional scholars and historians who have actually bothered to study the Second and Fourteenth Amendments, among them Joyce Lee Malcolm, author of *To Keep and Bear Arms: The Origins of an Anglo-American Right,* conclude that they were created to protect the citizen's right to arms. The three-volume *Gun Control and the Constitution,* edited by Robert J. Cottrol, assembles historical documents that are hard for gun control advocates to challenge. So they avoid them.

From the beginning there has been a racial aspect to the nation's gun laws, often masked by pieties about gun safety. Much has been written about this, but the subject has been avoided by liberals, seized on by Libertarians, and misused by the crazier right-wing gun advocates. (For objective writing on this subject, the papers of Malcolm and Cottrol are a good place to start.) The fact is that the right of every citizen to own a gun was taken for granted in this country until periodic race and immigration issues brought it into question. After the Civil War southern whites denied blacks the right to own guns. Consequently, race and gun ownership were factors in the ratifying of the Fourteenth Amendment in 1868. Besides nullifying the South's "black codes," which prohibited blacks from traveling, testifying in court, and suing whites, the amendment clearly guaranteed blacks the right of gun ownership and possession. This guarantee largely helped sell the passage of the Fourteenth Amendment to Congress. Supporters of Negro rights understood that an armed citizen "suffered significantly less likelihood of oppression"—shorthand for being lynched.

Ever-resourceful southerners, however, managed to keep blacks disarmed despite the Fourteenth Amendment. And by the early 1900s Negro-fearing southerners had a new ally in denying guns to minorities. Alarmed by the arrival of millions of immigrants, northern whites pushed to restrict access to guns through reinterpretation of the Second Amendment. Because of the amendment's odd structure (it almost seems to have been written off-the-cuff, as if the sense of it is so obvious it needs no comment or special consideration), they found reinterpreting the plainly worded main clause to be rough going. So they skipped over the main clause and latched on to a dependent clause referring to a state's relationship to "well-regulated militia" and began building a case for gun control from there.

By 1911 frightened New Yorkers had made progress. New York State passed the Sullivan Law, licensing weapons and making it a felony to conceal one. Then along came Al Capone, Baby Face Nelson, and John Dillinger, inspiring enough public fear and outrage to spawn the National Firearms Act of 1934, which controlled sawed-off long guns and automatic weapons.

Things stayed that way until the 1960s, when televised racial violence, the Kennedy and King assassinations, and rising crime rates scared the bejesus out of metro dwellers and not a few heartlanders. Conservatives in the cities bought guns or oiled up the ones they already owned. Smelling the spoor of a fresh but familiar breed of fearful voter, politicians called for government gun control. They got it in the form of the 1968 Gun Control Act, which, using the assassinations of King and the Kennedys as a rallying point, was ostensibly passed to eliminate gun violence. Antigun writers then and for a decade afterward were not as emotional as the antigun crowd today, and they pointed out the atmosphere of racial tension that spawned our gun control laws. Staunch antigun journalist and author Robert Sherrill *(The Saturday Night Special)* did not shrink from writing:

> The Gun Control Act of 1968 was passed not to control guns but to control blacks, and inasmuch as a majority of Congress did not want to do the former but were ashamed to show that their goal was the latter, the result was they did neither. Indeed, this law, the first gun control law passed by Congress in thirty years, was one of the grand jokes of our time. First of all, bear in mind that it was not passed in one piece but was a combination of two laws. The original 1968 Act was passed to control handguns after the Rev. Martin

Luther King, Jr., had been assassinated with a *rifle*. Then it was repealed and repassed to include the control of *rifles and shotguns* after the assassination of Robert F. Kennedy with a *handgun*. . . . The moralists of our federal legislature as well as sentimental editorial writers insist that the Act of 1968 was a kind of memorial to King and Robert Kennedy. If so, it was certainly a weird memorial, as can be seen not merely by the handgun/long-gun shellgame, but from the inapplicability of the law to their deaths.

The most enduring legacy of the era was gun lobbies. And more gun lobbies. Not to mention the rise of the NRA, which wrapped itself in the noble robe of Protector of the Second Amendment, a garment it had retrieved from the bottom of the La Brea Tar Pits, where it had been tossed by unknown parties and weighted down with a jukebox. Curiously, the robe bore an ACLU laundry mark.

By the end of the sixties the hunter in the deer stand in Iowa believed there were people—he wasn't sure who—who wanted to take away his gun and were challenging his rights under the Second Amendment. Although he didn't know exactly what the Second Amendment stood for, Republican politicians, conservative pundits, and wild-eyed Libertarians were more than happy to enlighten him. Today, it may be the only amendment he can recite. Anyway, the GOP was right there, gleefully bird-dogging the culprits, those urban liberals who'd never seen a 12-gauge or bought a deer license stamp. For once the GOP was right, and for forty years Republicans have been riding that same horse with great success.

* * *

Ed and Charlie are more on target than they know. For a decade criminological studies have demolished the cartoonishly over-simplified notion that people are more likely to kill a family member than they are to kill an intruder. To the contrary, the literature shows that self-protection weapons really do protect their owners. Among the many studies proving what no antigun lobbyist wants to hear are those of Florida State University criminologist Gary Kleck, whose research indicates that about two and a half million Americans successfully protect themselves with guns every year. Lest Kleck be written off as just another advocate, his methodology and conclusions were good enough to be utilized by the U.S. Government Accounting Office, an accomplishment rare for gun control groups. More than 2 million people are spared becoming crime victims because they own guns. Almost never do these cases involve firing the weapon. Displaying it and saying "Get the fuck out of here" seems to do the trick. If that doesn't work, a shot in the air does. Also disproved were the claims that every domestic fight and minor argument would turn into bloody shoot-outs. It just didn't happen. More than a million Americans are licensed to carry personal firearms, yet researchers find that misuse by this group has been statistically negligible.

Now that most states have passed laws allowing honest citizens to carry concealed weapons, gun advocates are being proven more right than they ever hoped to be. Joy of joys, it is women—in fact, poor urban women—and the poor in general who benefit most from concealed-carry laws. It doesn't get any better than that when it comes to serving up cold crow to Democratic gun controllers. Large declines in rapes and attacks on women have occurred wherever the laws have been enacted. A study by John R. Lott Jr., author of *More Guns, Less Crime: Understanding Crime and Gun-Control Laws,* found that the urban poor and minorities lived more safely with guns in their pockets or purses: "Not only do urban areas tend to gain in their fight against crime, but reductions in crime rates are greatest precisely in those urban areas that have the highest crime rates, largest and most dense populations, and greatest concentrations of minorities." Even though Lott is a bit too far right for my tastes, *More Guns, Less Crime* is a good book. Neither camp in the debate is made up primarily of liars, and both sides would do well to listen to one another once in a while.

Most liberal antigun advocates do not get off the city bus after working the second shift. Nor do they duck and dodge from street light to street light at 1 a.m. while dragging their laundry to the Doozy Duds, where they sit, usually alone, for an hour or so, fluorescently lit up behind the big plate-glass window like so much fresh meat on display, garnished with a promising purse or wallet, before they make the corner-to-corner run for home with their now-fragrant laundered waitress or fast-food uniforms. Barack Obama never did it. Hillary Clinton never did it. Most of white middle-class America doesn't do it either. The on-the-ground value of the Second Amendment completely escapes them.

The Second Amendment is the "Rodney Dangerfield of the Bill of Rights," as George Washington University law professor Robert J. Cottrol puts it. Cottrol—raised in Harlem, African American, and a self-described "Humphrey Democrat"—writes that it is the amendment most consistently attacked by editorial writers, demagoguing politicians, and the influential liberal elites. Especially the press. According to studies by press organizations, three-quarters of U.S. newspapers have advocated severely limiting gun ownership, stepping politely over the fact that the right to be armed is constitutionally guaranteed. The *Washington Post* probably holds the record, with seventy antigun pieces in seventy-seven days during the run-up to the passing of one of D.C.'s numerous gun control laws. The *Post* remained unflinching even when its gun control advocate columnist Carl Rowan shot a teenage trespasser taking a dip in his swimming pool with an unregistered 22-caliber long-range pistol. Rowan had recently called for "a complete and universal federal ban on the sale, manufacture, importation, and possession of handguns." He and the *Post* rolled along on the gun control wagon, with Rowan proclaiming his belief in strict gun control right up until his death in 2000.

When it comes to gun control, even credible sources such as the Government Accounting Office cannot get media coverage. What never makes the news are facts such as these from the National Institute of Justice (the research arm of the Department of Justice) and GAO reports on firearms:

> Citizens use guns to defend themselves against criminals as many as 2.5 million times every year—or about 6,850 times a day. Each year firearms are used sixty times more often to protect the lives of citizens than to take lives. The majority of these citizens defend themselves by brandishing their weapons or firing a warning shot. Citizens shoot and kill at

least twice as many criminals as police do every year (1,527 to 606). Only two percent of civilian shootings involved an innocent person mistakenly identified as a criminal. By constrast, the error rate for the police officers is eleven percent.

Approximately 200,000 women defend themselves against sexual abuse each year. The Carter Justice Department found that nationwide 32 percent of more than 32,000 attempted rapes were committed, but only 3 percent of the attempted rapes were successful when a woman was armed with a gun or knife.

Those facts are sure to generate a lot of *buts* from a misinformed public and to attract scorching criticism from "experts" whose academic or lobbying careers are built on gun control. I'm sure they will make arguments that sound quite convincing. But the fact remains that much of the conventional wisdom about guns is completely wrong.

Newspapers, radio, and television give the impression that school shootings and gun accidents among young children are increasingly common. The truth is they are both very rare and declining. More guns supposedly equals more violence, but over the past four decades, as the stock of civilian firearms rose by 262 percent, fatal gun accidents dropped by nearly 70 percent. People believe what they want to believe, even people who pride themselves on being more educated, rational, and objective than some yahoo nail banger dressed up like a Confederate at Fort Shenandoah in the Virginia woods. They seem unwilling to consider that their fervor over gun control may be rooted in their fear of people unlike themselves walking past them on the streets of their very own cities every day.

* * *

When darkness fell on Fort Shenandoah, I found myself where I hoped I would be, with several other campers around a fire playing music. A lifelong player of the guitar and recently the banjo, I'm always looking for an opportunity to play music with other human beings rather than with recordings or alone—making unadulterated, unamplified human sounds, particularly blues, minstrel music, and early mountain stuff. Keeping the world safe for living-room music. The fire was crackling and the bottle was going round. These were not the family guys. This was the drinking crowd, the guys come to party. We played the minstrel tune "Richmond Is a Hard Road to Travel" and a number of other Civil War period songs, then settled into things a tad more modern, which here means circa 1900. Along the way I told them that I was writing a book and that one chapter of it would be about guns.

"So I got a joke for your book," proffered Donny, whom I happened to already know, a wiry little fellow recently retired from the U.S. Navy and a soulful guitar player. "This fella goes into a gun shop and asks for a rifle with a scope. The owner hands him one and says: 'You can check it out by pointing it over that way toward my house. You should be able to see my wife.' The customer replies, 'All I see are a man and woman running around the house naked.' The owner takes the gun, looks through the scope, and hands it back to the customer along with two cartridges. 'If you use these two bullets on them you can have the gun for free, along with a lifetime supply of ammo.' The man looks through the scope, hands one of the bullets back to the owner, and says, 'I think I can get them both with just one shot.'"

One bottle of Jack Daniels later, just past midnight, we were into the music and the solo stuff—the time when each person does a couple of his best songs. I picked Robert Johnson's "Walking Blues." That nobody there had ever heard of the legendary bluesman Robert Johnson should have been a clue. I closed my eyes and leaned into the lyrics.

"Woke up this morning . . . uummm hummm . . . Felt around for my shoes . . . ummmmhum . . . Lord knows I got 'em . . . Got them mean old walking blues."

When I was done, I opened my eyes to a ring of hardened faces in the firelight. Donny said with a menacing look made especially ominous by the flickering fire, "When you sang that, your lips peeled back just like a blue-gummed jigaboo." The others seemed even less impressed than Donny. Needless to say, considering the company, I let that one go by. I had wandered into a clot of good-old-boy white Virginians of the type that is not supposed to exist anymore, according to the chamber of commerce and most Virginians.

But what I found far more interesting, chilling really, than their racism was the gun talk. Most of these men were military-gun aficionados and "personal weapons collectors." In other words, they bought and collected "antipersonnel firepower"—guns designed specifically to kill human beings. Without apology. America's relationship with its guns is no more written in black and white than any other, and this is one of the more disturbing fetishes to be found in some dark corners of the gun culture. Hundreds of thousands of American men, maybe a couple of million, no one knows for sure, are obsessed with the micro-mechanics of lethality—the nuts and bolts and screws of killing human beings. It would be cheating to leave them out of a discussion of armed America, though everyone seems to do just that—pretending they are not there or not aberrant. Of course, there are far fewer of them than there are ordinary American hunters. But they make up for their small numbers by their weirdness.

This single-minded focus on hardware is not exclusively American, but it is characteristically American. As a former senior editor at *Military History Magazine,* the largest in its category, I saw this growing American obsession with weaponry mechanics firsthand every working day. I continue to see in it the increasing militarization of our culture, the consequence perhaps of life in what more and more resembles a security state.

As I wrote earlier in this chapter, I couldn't care less about owning guns these days. I haven't fired a gun in at least sixteen years. But every once in a while, usually when I am experiencing extreme tension, an image zips through my mind that shows me how primitive and deeply rooted the psychological processes and emotions involved in the mechanics of lethality are. The image is that of myself killing somebody. The squeezing of the trigger, the muzzle blast, all in a split second. Then a feeling of relief. I am not alone in experiencing this flash of murderous imagery. Other American men experience the same, I have learned, though it is so deeply embedded in the unconscious that it takes a lot of discussion before they realize or admit that it does indeed happen.

I doubt that most white men raised in middle-class urban environments experience this unless they are combat veterans, which few of them are. I used to believe it was a product of boy-hoods spent hunting, imagining ourselves as Confederate sol-diers, cowboys and Indians, and, in my generation particularly, GIs fighting the Japanese and the Germans. And maybe it is. But I've met inner-city blacks and Latinos who experience the same flash of potency from the barrel of some unseen inner gun. In that moment we become Thanatos, the personification of death in Greek mythology. There's more to it than conditioning by movies and television, though that certainly plays a part. Perhaps it has something to do with America's violent frontier begin-nings. I am not sure, but I do know that many men have these mental flashes of violence involving a gun. It is much like the im-agery of small boys playing at war, only scarier. And there is something very American about it too, because I've never met a European who experiences this, though Bosnia might be a good place to look.

But getting back to the campfire at Fort Shenandoah, Glen, a retired military noncom of some sort, began regaling the campers with the word from his son, a Marine in Iraq. The kid loves it, he said, and just re-upped for another four years. For men like Glen, the Iraq War is as good as it gets, what with the public rise of military consciousness, the delivering of all Ameri-cans to the planet of the gun whether they want to go or not.

As he rated the U.S. weapons used in Iraq, Glen was as happy as a pig in the produce aisle: "The M16 rifle is pure dogshit. Jams in desert sand and you can't even count on the 5.56mm (.223) round to kill in a direct torso hit." (You, dear reader, are advised to use a different round on your next torso hit.) "The M2 .50-cal heavy machine gun. Whoa, Nelly! It puts 'em dick down in the dirt every time! The M14 with the light Kevlar stock? Great gun . . . got that low power red dot or ACOG sight. And *love* that 7.62 round! Then there is the night vision and infra-red equipment. Fantastic! Our guys see in the dark and *own* the night. The goat fuckers grub down and hide after evening prayers. U.S. hunter-killer teams rule! We've all seen the videos."

They surely have seen the videos. Even I have seen them. Brown heads explode in a pink bloody cloud, and half bodies with limbs askew sail through the air on a dozen or so videos circulating on the Internet—gruesome stuff shot through sniper scopes and cackled at over beers in dens around the country. Scarcely a month went by at *Military History Magazine* that I didn't receive a new video from some reader all jacked up over the war in Iraq. These bizarre care packages would be easier to dismiss if they came from uneducated greaseballs. But the average reader has an $80,000 household income, at least a bachelor's degree, and is usually well traveled. For example, I received videos regularly from a law professor in Oklahoma who assumed that because I edit a military history magazine, I must love this stuff.

Glen went on to describe the enemy: "The camel jocks are brave but stupid. . . . They will send a dozen men charging at our bases just to probe. Most of 'em get their asses greased, but they don't seem to mind. Survivors then run back to the same building they charged out of, hopped up and ready to make some kind of last stand. Our guys call these buildings AWRs—Allah's waiting rooms. All we do is bring down laser-guided ground air on 'em. Marine F-18s."

Incidentally, there was no mention in Glen's narrative of the fact that the Iraqis meet American technology with common sense and more American technology. When the newer armored-up Humvees were shipped into Iraq, the Iraqis simply fired RPGs through the windshield at point-blank range. At this writing, it's still not safe to drive anywhere; in fact, plain old driving is the most dangerous thing one can do in Iraq. Three 155mm artillery shells wired together and detonated with a cell phone takes care of a tank very handily. Maybe the strangest thing is the way Iraqis drop rockets and mortars on the American troops inside the U.S. bases. Using Google Earth and handheld GPS for over-head views of U.S. positions from about fifteen kilometers away, they launch rockets into the base while thousands of troops bluster and bristle at the gates.

Glen's creepy narrative had less to do with the realities of combat in Iraq and more to do with boasting about the warrior psyche and American technology. The people around that fire love the technology. They mentally caress every cartridge and enjoy the solid weight of the handguns under their coats. Nearly all of them have concealed-weapons permits. And nearly all of them have instabilities that would seem to make them a hazard with those weapons—usually unwarranted suspiciousness and anger toward authority. Media portrayals of a hyperdangerous America inflame these feelings. Despite their bravado, these men fear the greater world. To anyone unfamiliar with guns, it probably seems downright amazing they don't blow away the meter reader, or the neighbor's kid who crawls into their base-ment, or their girlfriend some drunken summer night. Such inci-dents happen but are extremely rare. Again, it appears that even the strangest gun-owning Americans have things under control when it comes to everyday gun safety.

Yet I shudder to think about what the Glens and the Donnys of the world will do if one day things spiral out of control. What happens when this country finally hits Peak Oil Demand and the electrical grid starts browning down and even little things become desperately difficult or unaffordable? What happens if the wrong kind of president declares the wrong kind of national emergency? What will be the first reflex of those hundreds of thousands of devotees of lethality?

Yesterday was one of those cold reflective southern winter days that make your heart ache in some indistinct way for things past. Maybe it's all that silver in the sky or the flash of eternity in the eyes of the pale children and old men on the porches. I don't know. But it caused me to drive out to the 1876 churchyard where Daddy is buried, then to the old homeplace on Shanghai Road, where I parked my truck and walked once more in the ridgefield where my father downed the deer so long ago. From there I can see Kenny Ray's trailer.

Cousin Kenny, who has been on the old family farm all his life, lives on a hilltop. A forty-foot flagpole in his front yard flies Old Glory and the eagle, globe, and anchor of the Marine Corps. He has one son in Iraq. He hunts alongside his other son and grandson in the ridgefield above Shanghai Road. And like the ghosts of those old men watching them as they hunt on what to us is hallowed ground, Ken and his boys are meat hunters. For them and tens of millions like them, guns will always be tools as ordinary and commonplace as a hammer or a cigarette lighter, yet endowed with the power of memory and the Devil's own fire.

For fifty years Kenny has oiled his guns and walked this ground, haunted by Pap, Daddy, Uncle Nelson, haunted by our Scots-Irish and Huguenot forefathers who likewise trod here, who planted it in buckwheat and hunted its frozen stubble. And when we hear that distant rifle crack, followed by the endlessly repeating echoes across the leafless ridges, we know the echoes are the sound of their guns bringing down a buck somewhere in heaven.

5

The Covert Kingdom

THEY PLEAD UPON THE BLOOD OF JESUS FOR A
THEOCRATIC STATE

The political movement we call the religious right, based largely
in fundamentalist churches, has deeply changed American
politics. Let's not kid ourselves: every person reading this will
be contending with it in many ways for the rest of their lives.
There will be no exceptions. —Fred Clarkson, *Eternal Hostility:
The Struggle Between Theocracy and Democracy*

The fellow perched on the lawn tractor giving me directions is huge. He wears a "Git 'er Done!" ball cap, a yellow nylon net T-shirt with tufts of chest hair sticking through, and camo flip-flops, and he weighs almost as much as the tractor itself. Its little black tires smush deeper into the wet sod as he speaks: "Yew go raht down heer two blocks past the trailer court and tern left on Dale Earnhardt Lane." Only in the American South could you get such a set of directions from such an unlikely character. (Doubters are invited to enter "Dale Earnhardt Lane, 25401" into Yahoo! Maps.) I am sure some readers are smirking at a class of people who would name a street after a guy whose main achievement was driving in a circle at 200 miles per hour for years on end until he finally bit the big one. Some unsympathetic souls would say, "That's what you get, you damned dumb motherfucker." But not me. As a liberal (ahem!), I revere life.

The fact that I have to ask directions to the church where my younger brother is a pastor is some indicator of how often I attend services. Nevertheless, Brother Mike warmly embraces me when I do manage to show up at Shenandoah Bible Baptist Church. Shenandoah Bible is not a megachurch, but it's large as local praise temples go, with more than a thousand members and some two hundred children enrolled in its fundamentalist Christian school. Built in that featureless architectural style of the 1960s, this wheat-colored brick-and-glass structure sitting in an expanse of green could be part of any of the low, spread-out office campuses so common in this country, were it not for the three steel crosses creating a slim spire at the top.

Brother Mike has been preacher, youth pastor, bus outreach manager, and general all-round wrangler for God at this church since 1974. That was the year Patty Hearst was kidnapped by the Symbionese Liberation Army, Nixon resigned, and Brother Mike was born-again in Christ. For thirty of the thirty-one years since then, he and his wife June lived in a church-supplied mobile home on the church property. Only in 2006, with retirement staring them in the face, did they move into a middle-class ranch house of their own, again with help from the church.

My brother's church is what is known as an independent Baptist church. It is independent enough of your world and mine that he says things like, "I helped cast out a demon the other day, Joey. I wish you could have been there." Independent fundamentalist churches are theologically wooly places whose belief systems can accommodate just about any interpretation of the Good Book that a "Preacher Bob" or a "Pastor Donnie" can come up with. Members of the clergy arise from within the church ranks and are usually poorly educated, though, like most Americans, they do not see themselves that way. Lack of a broad higher education is a hallmark of fundamentalist ministers and goes completely unremarked by their congregations, in whose eyes a two-year technical school or community college, and especially a seminary of their own, is on par with nearly any of the vile secular universities. In fact, the "Bible colleges" are *better* because they don't teach philosophy, science, the arts, or literature in any form a secular person would recognize.

This rejection of "fancy learnin'" has been a feature of American fundamentalism since the backwoods-stump church days, and it continues to provide the nation with charismatic literalists whose analytical abilities are minimal. If you combine that with more than thirty years of Christian school growth (rooted in the antidesegregation movement), more than 2 million fundamentalist Christian school students nationally, and millions more fundamentalist kids in the public school system, you can begin to understand why so many states find themselves revamping their educational systems so that the teachings of Darwin can be replaced by the fables of Adam and Eve and we can all be reassured that David slew Goliath despite the complete lack of evidence that either existed.

The members of Shenandoah Bible Baptist are ultraright politically, though they don't think so. They consider themselves "mainstream," and if numbers tell the story, they have a better claim to that label than the liberals whom they outnumber.

Being very certain that God exists is a mainstream characteristic. Seventy-six percent of Protestants, 64 percent of Catholics, and one-third of Jews are "absolutely certain," according to Harris polls. The members of Shenandoah Bible are also in the mainstream when it comes to their level of education. They are among the three-quarters of Americans who seem satisfied just to finish high school or who think that a year or so of any sort of training after high school is enough. (Liberals can be grateful they are not all registered voters. As it stands, Christian fundamentalists make up 25 percent of those entitled to vote, according to the Pew Research Center, and 20 million of America's 50 million fundamentalists voted in the last two elections.)

Pollsters agree that church attendance is among the best indicators of whether a voter is liberal or conservative. Sixty-two percent of working-class Americans attend church, and 89 percent of all Americans take their faith seriously enough to make it to church several times a year. Thirty-six percent of them attend church at least twice a month.

Gallup surveys show that one-quarter to one-third of the U.S. population identifies itself as "born-again" evangelicals, a large umbrella that includes liberal born-agains such as Jimmy Carter and even a few Christian Greens. There is more diversity among fundamentalists than is generally understood by the secular public. But taken as a whole, fundamentalists have three things in common: They are whiter than Aunt Nelly's napkin, and, for the most part, they are working class and have only high school educations.

Yet some evangelicals stand apart from the mainstream in one important way: They would scrap the Constitution and institute "Biblical Law," the rules of the Old Testament, and they take the long view toward the establishment of a theocratic state. Others believe we are rapidly entering the End Times and the fulfillment of the darkest biblical prophecies. Like many of their Scots-Irish ancestors, they see a theocracy of one sort or another as a necessary part of the End Times, and, though few publicly say so, some are not averse to a nuclear war in the Middle East, ideally with the help of Israel.

As Brother Mike puts it, "Israel is the key to everything. When the state of Israel was founded, the End Times were set in motion." To wit, the Messiah can return to earth only after an apocalypse in Israel called Armageddon, which a minority of influential fundamentalists are promoting with all their power so that The End can take place. The first requirement was establishment of the state of Israel. Done. The next is Israel's occupation of the Middle East as a return of its "Biblical lands." Which means more wars. Radical Christian conservatives believe that peace cannot ever lead to Christ's return, and indeed impedes the thousand-year Reign of Christ, and that anyone promoting peace is a tool of Satan. Fundamentalists support any and all wars Middle Eastern, and many consider the deaths of their own children as a kind of holy martyrdom. "He (or she) died protecting this country's Christian values." You hear it over and over from the most radical parents of those killed. The parade of deaths, however, has shaken at least a few loose from the militaristic Christian fold.

End Times theology, or premillennialism (a once obscure doctrine conceived by John Nelson Darby of the Plymouth Brethren in 1827), has many variants. All of them boil down to the idea that history is scripted by God and will soon come to an apocalyptic conclusion according to his plan. Your only hope is to accept Jesus as your personal Savior. Then, if you happen to be a member of the Rapturist cult of End Times believers, God will "rapture you up" just as he launches seven years of horror and death upon the earth. An Antichrist will arise, and worldwide war will be the norm. Billions will die. Fundamentalist Christians look around at AIDS, warfare across the globe, crime, the rise of narco-states, and ecological collapse, and they see confirmation of God's plan. Rev. Rich Lang of Trinity United Methodist Church in Seattle says, "This theology of despair is very seductive and it is shaping the spirituality of millions of Christians today."

Hard-core End Times fundamentalists apply their interpretation of the Bible to all things in life, including modern world politics, with predictably strange conclusions:

- The United Nations is a tool of the Antichrist. America alone must spread the gospel around the world.
- There is no need to worry about the environment because we are not going to need this earth much longer.
- Israel is to be defended at all costs and even encouraged to expand, because the Bible declares that Israel must rule all the land from the Nile to the Euphrates in order for End Times prophecy to be fulfilled.
- God will provide a Christian leader to shepherd the American flock as they become his chosen people to extend the gospel worldwide and rid the earth of evil.

Meanwhile, there is the work of "reconstructing" our country and achieving "dominion" over it, as required by certain core End Times theologies. "Reconstructionist" plans are as hard and unforgiving as a gravestone. Capital punishment, central to the Reconstructionist ideal, is prescribed for a wide range of crimes, including abandonment of the faith, blasphemy, heresy, witchcraft, astrology, adultery, sodomy, homosexuality, striking a parent, and "unchastity before marriage" (by women only).

Biblically correct methods of execution include stoning, the sword, hanging, and burning. Stoning is preferred, according to Gary North, self-styled Reconstructionist economist, because stones are plentiful and cheap. Biblical law would also eliminate labor unions, civil rights laws, and public schools. The late Reconstruction theologian David Chilton declared, "The Christian goal for the world is the universal development of Biblical theocratic republics."

Incidentally, the Republic of Jesus as described by some End Times cults would be not only a legal hell but an ecological one as well. Pure Rapturist doctrine (all types of Rapturists argue over whose doctrine is purest) calls for scrapping environmental protection of all kinds, because there will be no need for this planet once the Rapture occurs.

You may not have heard of Reconstructionists such as R. J. Rushdoony or David Chilton or Gary North. But individually and together they have influenced more contemporary American minds than Noam Chomsky, Gore Vidal, and Howard Zinn combined. Christian Reconstructionism and Dominionism are by no means the dominant strains of fundamentalism these days, nor have they ever been. But since the 1970s, through hundreds of books and college classes, the doctrine of Reconstructionism has come to permeate not only the religious right but mainstream churches as well, through demonstrative Charismatic movements such as Pentecostalism, which focuses on healing, prophecy, and gifts such as the ability to "speak in tongues." Pentecostals lined up behind Christian media mogul Pat Robertson in the 1970s and 1980s, making him rich and powerful. In return, he gave them the power and confidence to launch emotionally and politically charged movements such as the effort to overturn *Roe v. Wade* (thereby elevating the humble zygote into previously unimaginable news value).

This push toward a theocracy and the infiltration of mainstream Protestantism by religious extremists was one of the biggest underreported political stories of the second half of the twentieth century. Religious reporters all but ran from it, partly because they must please all the churches they cover. But many of them didn't even see it happening. Yet thousands of mainstream Methodist, Presbyterian, and other Protestant churches were pushed inexorably rightward, often without even realizing it. Clearly the Methodist church down the street from my house does not understand what it has become. Other mainstream churches with more progressive leadership flinched and bowed to the radicals at every turn. They had to if they wanted to retain or gain members swept up in the evangelical movement. So what if the most fervent of these people declared that lesbianism was rampant in the nation's middle school restrooms and vowed to reconstruct America to fit Leviticus?

Pastor Jeff Owens has just begun the announcements when I scoot into the rearmost pew of Shenandoah Bible Baptist Church. "All men who want to go to the big gun show and shooters' exposition in Claysburg sign up for the bus after service," he says. "Men ten years old and older who want to get certified in gun safety meet in the Persian Room." He goes on to announce the Young Fundamentalist meeting and the Adult and

Teen "Soul-Winning" meeting. Also on the menu are gender-segregated events such as "It's a Girl Thing!" (for girls thirteen to eighteen years old) and "Singspiration Around the Bonfire" (ladies only). It's a busy place.

Pastor Jeff is one of those unnervingly wholesome, spotlessly groomed fundamentalists, the kind with the relentlessly zappy 300-volt smile that borders on hysteria. He's always psyched, eyes ever alert, presumably for souls to save. Pastor Jeff preaches in the old style, growing increasingly loud as the sermon progresses. What his voice lacks in sonorousness, he makes up for in exclamation and exhortation, and he hammers his lines over and over using a southern technique that has served everyone from Martin Luther King to Oral Roberts: repetition and rhythm.

"*To me* there are no little problems," he tells the congregation. "*To me* there are no little matters in this life." The litany of things that are not little to Pastor Jeff lasts a full minute, and in the end "*To me*" is far more deeply ingrained than the list of things that are not so little. Yet each item on the list seems to hit home with listeners. "*To me* there are no little Christian watch nights, because on the most ordinary nights one of our daughters' virginity might be saved. And *to me* there are no little problems and no little people . . . no poor people. . . . The richest people here tonight [as if there were any rich people in the congregation] have not the value of the widow's mite. Have not as much worth in God's eyes as those of you who put one dollar in the plate. *To me* you can never be little or lost or insignificant because *to God* you can never be little. *There are no little things in this world.* No little deeds, no little sins, no little acts of kindness, and *no little people here tonight!*"

This message of worthiness is balm to those who do the thankless work of this world and suffer the purest snub of all: invisibility. Most people here tonight do not have careers; they have jobs, and they exist as part of the background of the lives of the professional and semiprofessional middle classes. After all, somebody has to groom the dogs and wire the doctor's new $60,000 kitchen. Somebody has to collect all the quarters from the Laundromats and drive the semitrailers to the Pottery Barn warehouse.

Meanwhile, the plate is smoothly passed and Pastor Jeff slips into the offering pitch. The variety of these pitches never ceases to amaze. "God is generous with you *every* day! Right?" Now thankful for the simple drawing of breath, everyone replies, "*Yes!* Praise him!" "Therefore," yells Pastor Jeff, "why are you so stingy on this occasion to repay him?" There is a roar of agreement. A sign on the wall shows that the church members put their money where their mouth is: It says SBBC has donated one and a half million dollars for missionary work, a hefty chunk of change for working folks.

The congregation mumbles along behind the choir in a hymn. One thing is certain: Nobody ever came to this or to any modern fundamentalist church for the music. The mushy new music strives to sound as un-hymnlike as possible and succeeds. It is bland, with predictable, graceless melodies and awkward notes thrown in occasionally to make the songs sound complex and "composed." Only a church music director or a Christian publishing company could love it. This morning's selections are somewhat less bland than usual; they include a rather strange song that is a mixture of childish singsong and gory imagery, with lyrics such as "Jesus used me as a canvas and He signed it at the bottom with His name in blood." Shenandoah Bible Baptist is not one of your guitar-and-drums-up-front-beside-the-pulpit Pentecostal churches. It is more representative of the churches of heartland America's truck drivers, bookkeepers, small contractors, tire mechanics, bank tellers, and grocery clerks—holders of the disposable jobs in our insecure new economy.

Those working people have plenty of reasons to feel economically insecure because they take it in the shorts whenever Wall Street gets moody. Still, they claim to believe they have an equal shot at being as successful as anyone else in America, despite the fact that they are merely interchangeable parts in the American production and service machinery. They are good cogs and show great deference toward any type of authority. At work many are treated like children. For example, companies in these parts require employees to bring in written notes from doctors if they use their sick days. The first time a medical receptionist asked me if I wanted "a written excuse from the doctor for your boss," I thought I'd heard her wrong and asked her to repeat it.

Fundamentalist religion demands gratitude for what God grants. So these people are grateful to be earning three bucks above minimum wage: "After all, aren't we better-off than our parents were?" Maybe, but most of their parents had health insurance and got by without both spouses having to work. They own more "stuff" than their parents ever had. They pay more for a pair of brand-name sneakers for their children than their parents paid for an entire month's groceries. So if the number on the paycheck is bigger than in former times and the house is full of gadgets, well, they figure they have plenty for which to be grateful even if they do have to buy groceries with a credit card from time to time. People are starving in India, right? Judging from the wall-to-wall double-wide rumps in the pews, no one is starving here. God provides Big Macs and supermarket bakery cakes. There's plenty to be grateful for, but more than anything else, there is being a part of this church community. Unlike public schools or civic organizations, the fundamentalist church is one of the few social structures still functioning in America, and it welcomes everyone, rich or poor, good or bad.

If you look across the congregations of these churches, you will see these certainly aren't bad people—just working stiffs whose interior lives were clobbered by the late twentieth century. Theirs is part of the global revival of fundamentalism that occurred when materialism rose triumphant in the wake of the Enlightenment. (Poor dear Enlightenment! So brief! Then smashed by two world wars, Verdun, Dresden, Auschwitz, the gulags, nuclear weapons, and now impending ecological disaster.) Two generations of them were raised in Christian schools amid the unyielding hostility and fear stoked by the Cold War. Is it any wonder they are so drawn to the Apocalypse? From home as they know it in this nation, they look out the window and what they see does look like the end of the world.

Middle-of-the-road Jews, Unitarians, Protestants, and Catholics, not to mention the secular humanists among us, cannot imagine how complete a lifestyle the cultish fundamentalist churches provide. This self-referential culture is so focused on religion and conviction that it was bound to come to see the larger secular society as its persecutor and all authority other than God's, especially that of the government, as corrupt. There is not much they can do about the fact that so many Americans prefer the Sunday sports page to two hours of Bible study on "The Stick of Ephraim." But they discovered they *could* do something about the government: Infiltrate it. "Train up the Joshua Generation."

Fundamentalist strategists make it clear in their writings that the purpose of homeschooling and Christian academies is to create the right-wing Christian cadres of the future. The goal is to place ever-increasing numbers of believers in positions of governmental influence. "The apathy of other Americans can become a blessing and advantage to Christians," wrote Mark A. Beliles and Stephen K. McDowell in *America's Providential History,* one of the major textbooks of the Christian homeschool movement. Now we find the Joshua Generation replacing federal judges with fundamentalist Christians and putting them into law firms, banks, police forces, and the military as "faith-based force multipliers" for God's coming Christian rule.

The training of Christian cadres is far more sophisticated than nonfundamentalists realize. By now, most informed people probably know that the homeschoolers have a university network, with dozens of campuses across the nation, each with its own smiling Christian pod people, each school a clone of Jerry Falwell's Liberty University in Lynchburg, Virginia. But how many outsiders know the depth and specificity of political indoctrination in these schools?

For example, Patrick Henry College in Purcellville, Virginia, a college exclusively for Christian homeschoolers, offers programs in strategic government intelligence, law, and foreign policy, all with a strict, Bible-based "Christian worldview." Patrick Henry is so heavily funded by the Christian right it can offer classes below cost.

Seven percent of all internships handed out by the Bush administration went to Patrick Henry students, and many more went to graduates of similarly religious rightist colleges. The administration also recruited from the faculties of these schools, appointing right-wing Christian activist Kay Coles James, former dean of the Robertson School of Government at Pat Robertson's Regent University, as director of the U.S. Office of Personnel Management. What better position from which to recruit fundamentalists? Scratch any of these supposed academics and you are likely to find a Christian zealot. I know because I have made the mistake of inviting a few of these folks to cocktail parties. One university department head told me he is moving to rural Mississippi where he can better re-create the lifestyle of the antebellum South and its "Confederate Christian values."

Meanwhile, when the Rapture comes, Christians with the right credentials will fly away. But you and I, dear reader, will probably be among those who suffer a thousand-year plague of boils. So stock up on antibiotics because, according to the "Rapture Index," the end is near. See for yourself at www.raptureready. com. Part novelty, part obsession, the index is described as the "Dow Jones industrial average of end-time activity" and a "prophetic speedometer." It tracks forty-five categories—among them false Christs, plagues, inflation, beast government, and ecumenism—and assigns points to each indicating how predictive of the Rapture it is. As I write this, the index stands at 160, perilously close to critical mass, when people like us will be smitten under a sky filled with deliriously happy naked flying Christians.

It's easy to ridicule the notion of the Rapture—the time when God takes up all saved Christians before he lets loose slaughter, pestilence, and torture upon the earth—but I have lived with it as the backdrop of my entire life. My own father believed in the Rapture until the day he died, and the last time I saw him alive we talked about it. He asked me, "Will you be saved? Will you be there with me on Canaan's shore?" I feigned belief in it to give a dying man solace. But that was the spiritual stuff of families, and living and dying, religion in its rightful place, the way it is supposed to be, personal and intimate—not political.

Watching Brother Mike from the back row as he goes about his work down front of the church—all those graceful tasks preachers and associate preachers do when they are not sermonizing—one would never guess that he is at the center of a national storm. At fifty-eight, he is intelligent and sensitive looking in that manly way one sees in Levitra commercials and on the golf course—that affluent suburban look. I think about his Dominionist views, and I wonder whether the gracefully graying man with the Levitra smile would stone a homosexual if the harshest sort of Dominionism were to triumph. I sort of doubt it. But then I never thought I'd see the day when he cast out demons either.

Brother Mike understands that he and his flock are at a pivotal point in modern political history, although they would put it in terms of the hand of Satan or demons afoot in the world. Yet he seems to be a happy man, even as I toss and turn anxiously over the state of things. He would say that my soul is troubling me and that I need to be washed in the blood and redeemed by the grace of him who bled for our sins. I'd say that I am troubled by the distinct impression of approaching trihorned fascism— part Christian, part military, part corporate.

Our roads diverged forty years ago when I escaped the Christian environment to eat LSD, consider Buddhism, and let a couple of marriages go to hell. Eventually, to my family's amazement and relief, I managed to come to rest with a far better woman than I deserve, two dogs, and blood pressure high enough to keep me a respectable distance from the scotch bottle.

Whether I laugh or cry over this chasm between brothers, we end all our meetings and phone calls with the words "I love you." And we do love each other. And I can see Mike's genuine pain that I am not saved. One more time I, the prodigal brother, snatched from proffered grace by pride's certain hand pulling me back into its own dominion, back across the waters of Babylon, a river so deep and wide even blood and brotherhood cannot breach it. Who am I to say that hand is not the hand of a demon?

I am snatched from these reveries by Pastor Jeff's remarks to the congregation on God's relationship with ugly women. He tells a joke: A drunk says to a woman in a checkout line, "I can tell that you're single." "How?" she asks. "Because of the items I purchased?" "No, because you're ugly," the drunk replies. Pastor Jeff adds, "Plenty of you ladies in our congregation can be thankful that there are no ugly women in the eyes of God!"

Now there is a line you will never hear in the sermons of your average rabbi or priest. As in, "Hello, folks, and a special howdy to all you ugly women out there. God loves ya anyway!"

Finally comes the altar call to be saved. Tonight about a dozen people get saved, and as usual most of the respondents are teenagers. This is in no way surprising; at least half the people I know have been saved a couple of times. The first time around it's probably thanks to teenage hormones. The next time it might be courtesy of the divorce. But all will be baptized in the backlit artificial stone dunking pool behind the podium, which is standard in churches where members must "go under" for baptism to be legitimate. Churches are now too sophisticated to baptize God's children in God's rivers. The rivers are too polluted and lack a sound and video system. But I can remember back to the baptisms in the Shenandoah River, and much as I may seem a heathen today, I would give anything to go down to some shaded old riverbank singing and shouting at a good footwashing Baptist three-times-under baptism—some place that smells like bass leaping in the cool riverine haze while big old snapping turtles watch from a sunny rock offshore.

I would also someday like to watch Brother Mike or Pastor Jeff cast out the aforementioned demons. But a good exorcism—a word Baptists dislike for its taint of Catholicism—can't just be summoned with the snap of the fingers. About the only way I am likely to experience a Baptist exorcism is to be the object of one.

After the worship service, I approach Brother Mike about exorcism: "I gotta ask you, Brother Mike," I said, "do you cast out demons often?"

I must say here that one of the biggest quandaries in writing this book is that people trust me not to make fools of them. Brother Mike talks straight and is never evasive. It's the trust of a brother.

"I've encountered demons no more than six times in my life," he said. "I've only had a couple of direct casting-out experiences. But I think there are a lot more demons around that we do not recognize. Remember the maniac of Gadarenes? The guy in the Bible who was running around naked in the graveyard with two thousand demons in him? He's in the Bible twice: Mark 5:1 and Luke 8:26. Jesus cast the demons into a herd of swine. My most recent casting-out was in a young man twenty years old. His dad had come to me and said he thought his son was demon possessed. The boy was involved in drugs and sex. Drug dealers are sorcerers, part of Satan's power of the air now ruling here on earth to a large extent. Revelation 8 shows the connection."

"What do you do? Lay on hands or what?"

"We use scripture read aloud. Particularly those scriptures on the blood of Christ. The Devil hates the blood of Christ, and God promised the power in the blood. This young man said he could actually lie in bed and feel his girlfriend in his arms even though she wasn't there. He liked wild music, drink, and drugs. He talked to me for two hours, and all the time he had this dark look about him. So I looked into his eyes and said: 'I think you are demon possessed. Do you think you are? Do you think you have demons?' He said yes. I told him, 'Then you cannot get victory.'"

"Hell, little brother. What does a demon do when you try to cast him out?"

"Well, these demons never talked back to me, though sometimes they do. We started to pray, and the boy got up and ran. I pinned him to the door, and he started to growl at me just like a wild dog. And so here's what I did: I just plead the blood. The name of Christ has power, and the blood is where the real power is. After he calmed down a little, we sat him back in the chair, and his dad went to get two other preachers. We surrounded the boy and began to pray. He growled and tried again to run. We held him down in the chair for about twenty minutes or so, all three of us praying at the same time. We prayed loud. When you are fighting a spiritual battle like that, it gets real loud. Finally he went limp, and I think that is when the demon left. After that he was exhausted. He later got saved. That was several years ago, and he's still in the church."

"After an ordeal like that, I'll bet he is!"

Brother Mike tells me that Satan has an invisible army of demons doing his bidding and that every demon is different. He says demons will take up residence in a house and stay there for years.

"Me and Preacher [the church's founder] and two other guys cleared demons out of my son's father-in-law's house. Demons were exposing themselves to my son's father-in-law [who is, incidentally, a well-placed U.S. government administrator]. A black form with red eyes actually came into the room and stood over the bed. It scared the wife and kids to death. We got out the Book of Hebrews, chapters 9 and 10, where it talks about the blood and the victory. We went into every room and commanded the demons to leave in the name of Christ. We asked them to reveal themselves. We called them cowards in the face of God. They never came back."

"Geesh! The Baptist church has certainly gotten livelier since the days when I went to church."

I often make light here of millions of Americans whose magical thinking about the Bible resembles Dungeons and Dragons more than religious contemplation. I have to. It helps me deal with the fact that my own family believes in demons. Of course, my brother and I both care deeply about each other, though even as graying older men we still have great difficulty expressing it.

He is about to retire from the church, and I am still a bit surprised my little brother is a preacher at all, though I shouldn't be. We have any number of "brush preachers" in our family tree, Pentecostals and Baptists mainly. Pictures of them hang along my staircase, men like Great-Great Grandpa Baldwin, an angry-looking skinny old man with spectacles, dressed in a white suit and posed with legs crossed on a southern lawn, under trees, sitting on a straight-backed chair—and as always, with a Bible in his lap. And my parents did meet at a Billy Graham tent revival during the Second World War, marrying shortly afterward. The fact that I was born less than nine months after they married testifies to the Reverend Graham's charisma.

Sometimes I look at the framed photo of Great-Great Grandpa Baldwin, a Holiness Pentecostal preacher. My mother and her siblings hid under the bed when they saw his cadaverous white-suited frame approaching along the dusty road through the scrub pines. He was a carpenter—a damned good one on those occasions when he could find an employer who could stand to be around him. He sometimes killed copperhead snakes with his cane as he walked the roads with his Bible and muttered that they were "adders in the path of the righteous." According to family legend, he once took his cane to a woman who refused to quit pumping water from a well on a Sunday, and in his sermons he advocated that Christians band together and wage open war on nonbelievers. He never invited sinners to the altar to be saved (not that any nonbeliever would have had the balls to attend one of his services). Tar-and-feather the flappers, he said, and hang the bootleggers. Family members now long dead used to tell me that he saw Warren G. Harding as the Devil's disciple because Harding supported women's suffrage and had "nigger blood." Some of them agreed with him.

Looking at his photograph, I think to myself: You've finally done it. It took four generations, but you've finally goddamned done it. Gotten that war against reason and uppity secularists you always wanted. Gotten even for the Scopes trial, which they say was one of the many burrs under your saddle until your last breath. Well, rejoice, old man, because your tribes have gathered around America's oldest magical hairball of ignorance and superstition, Christian fundamentalism, and their numbers have enabled them to suck so much oxygen out of the political atmosphere that they are now acknowledged as a mainstream force in politics. Episcopalians, Jews, and affluent suburban Methodists and Catholics, they are all now scratching their heads, sweating, and swearing loudly that this pack of lower-class zealots cannot possibly represent the mainstream—not the mainstream they learned about in their fancy sociology classes or were so comfortably reassured about by media commentators who were people like themselves. Goodnight, Grandpa Baldwin. I'll toast you from hell.

You don't need a degree in sociology to see that the most obvious class indicator in America is religious belief and that religious zeal is concentrated in lower-class and working-class whites. One look at Brother Charlie casting a demon out of a Camaro engine block tells the story. Working-class whites have always been evangelical Protestants, and cartoons and newspaper stories depicting unruly lower-class religious fervor, spirit-filled altar calls, and manipulating or raving evangelist preachers can be found as far back as the 1820s. It was seen then as hick folly and still is, and the places where it flourishes, the places where millions of working Americans live, are still viewed as low class. Less than desirable. Paul Fussell puts it very nicely in his book *Class: A Guide Through the American Status System:*

> Another way to judge a place's undesirability is to measure the degree to which religious fundamentalism is identified with it. Akron, Ohio . . . is fatally known as the home of the Rex Humbard Ministry, the way Greenville, South Carolina, is known as the seat of Bob Jones University, and Wheaton, Illinois, is identified with Wheaton College and remembered thus as the forging ground of the great Billy Graham. Likewise Garden Grove, California, locus of the Rev. Robert Schuller,

famous for his automatic smile and his cheerful Cathedral of glass. Can a higher-class person live in Lynchburg, Virginia? Probably not, since that town is the origin of Dr. Jerry Falwell's radio emissions, the site of his church and the mailing address for free-will offerings. Indeed, it seems that no high-class person can live in any place strongly associated with religious prophecy or miracle.

By that standard there can be absolutely no hope for Winchester, Virginia. No cultured person with more than two fingers of forehead could possibly live enjoyably on an intellectual plane. On a simple four-block walk to the tavern, I pass two Pentecostal outfits, the Second Chance Church, and an "Institute for the Study of Creation Science" with television sets tuned into God on display in a front window and with its speakers bellowing the creationist message to passersby:

> If primates gave birth to creatures that gave birth to human beings, then why aren't they still doing it? Why aren't we seeing primates giving birth to man-apes today? Look around. See any? Of course not. There's the disproof of evolution right before your eyes!

How on earth could anyone accept such evolution as ape sex versus logic, much less foist it on other people? Of course millions of them were actually taught that in Christian schools back when they were little Joshuas. But many millions more who never set foot in a Christian school accept it because it sounds to them like a good scientific argument. Plus it is easy to understand

and supports their resentment of egghead scientists, who are too damned smart-assed anyway.

This is a uniquely American form of ignorance. With about half of all Americans ranging from minimally literate to functionally illiterate, truth falls before the scythe of rumor and the lust for spectacle. These Americans have eyes, which is to say the camera to shoot what is around them, but they have no intellectual software to edit or make sense of it all. Thus we find millions of fundamentalists producing their own mind movies of American reality, in which the secretary general of the United Nations is the Antichrist and the "Clinton crime family" deals in cocaine and is linked to the Gambino family. In these movies abortion doctors are microwaving and eating fetuses, according to testimony given by antiabortionists before a Kansas House subcommittee, and crowds of good folks get teary-eyed as Rev. Pat Evans of the NASCAR "Racing for Jesus Ministries" rumbles onto the track. Evangelical NASCAR? Yup. ABC called it America's "unapologetically evangelical sport." I can see you, dear reader, running and holding your head and screaming at the thought. Yet it's true. At Bristol and Talladega the earth is shaking for Jaaaayzus!

Pappy Baldwin, you may be relishing the triumph of ignorance and the clamor of the righteous rabble for the lynching of Darwin's ghost yet one more time. But they are having far too much fun at Talladega, aren't they? Tough beans, because nobody can stop ignorant folks from having ignorant fun and spectacle, which is pretty much the only kind of fun and spectacle available in this country. Still, you'd be proud of the clan of Joshuas who sprang from your loins, proud of the grisly and indelible promise of the Rapture you stamped on your descendants, me among them.

One September day when I was in the third grade, I got off the school bus and walked up the red dust–powdered lane to my house only to find no one there. The smudgy white front door of the old frame house stood open. My footsteps on the unpainted gray porch creaked in the fall stillness. With increasing panic, I went through every room and then ran around the outside of the house sobbing, in the grip of the most horrific loneliness and terror. I believed with all my heart that the Rapture had come and that all my family had been taken up to heaven, leaving me alone on earth to face God's terrible wrath. As it turned out, they were at a neighbor's house scarcely three hundred yards down the road and returned in a few minutes. But it took me hours to calm down. I dreamed about it for years afterward.

Since then I have spoken to others raised in fundamentalist families who had the same childhood experience of coming home and thinking everyone had been "raptured up." The Rapture is very real to people in whom its glorious and grisly promise has been instilled and cultivated since birth. Even those who escape fundamentalism agree its marks are permanent. We may no longer believe in being raptured up, but the grim fundamentalist architecture of the soul stands in the background of our days. An apocalyptic starkness remains somewhere inside us, one that tinges all our feelings and thoughts of higher matters. Especially about death, oh beautiful and terrible death, for naked eternity is more real to us than to those born into secular humanism.

Over the past few years I've received mail from hundreds of folks like me, the different ones who fled and became lawyers and teachers and therapists and car mechanics, dope dealers and stockbrokers and waitresses. And every one of them has felt that fearful emptiness, that inner lightning illuminating the carnage of lost souls, in the face of which we are meaningless and can only plead upon the blood of Jesus.

Pleading upon the blood of Jesus. I never heard that expression while growing up. Scary as biblical language seemed then, there is something more ominous about today's fundamentalist terminology. Close observers of conservative American Christianity know that it has grown darker and more blood oriented over the past few decades. Sermons speak of "pleading the blood of Jesus," "blood redemption," and "doctrine of the blood." As Diane Christian, professor of English at the State University of New York at Buffalo, wrote, "There is a big leap from the liberation of Exodus, when Jews sprinkled blood on their doorposts, to the salvation proposed by Christians, in which blood is drunk by a community of faith. The Christian community not only lives after death by the blood of their Christ; but they feed on it in life. What can this mean, to drink blood?"

It is a safe guess that it does not mean turn the other cheek.

I had dinner with Brother Mike's family back around the time the television networks were showing the dismembered U.S. civilian bodies strung up on the bridge at Fallujah and Mel Gibson's bloody Christ was hanging in agony in every movie house in the country. The overwrought emotionalism of these and other media blood offerings of the week coincided approximately with the Easter season, if I remember correctly. Not a word about it was spoken among my family and fundamentalist friends as far as I know, at least not to me. No one needed to. Brother Mike's children and wife and everyone else in their world were in complete agreement about what needed to be done in the Holy Land. They knew their president would take care of matters. Fallujah soon enough got its horrific payback for those TV images—and got it with the unconditional support of the Bageant family and the Shenandoah Bible Baptist Church.

Only another liberal raised in a fundamentalist clan can understand what a strange, sometimes downright hellish circumstance it is—how such a family can despise everything you believe in, see you as a humanist instrument of Satan, yet still love you and be right there for you when your back goes out or a divorce shatters your life. How they can never fail to invite you to the family's Thanksgiving dinner.

It must be plain that I do not find much conversational fat to chew around the Thanksgiving table. Politically and spiritually, my family and I may be said to be dire enemies. Love and loathing coexist. There is talk but no communication. At times it seems we are speaking to one another through an unearthly veil, wherein each party knows it is speaking to an alien. There is a sort of high, eerie, mental whine in the air. This is the sound of mutually incomprehensible worlds hurtling toward destiny, passing with great psychological friction, obvious to all yet acknowledged by none.

After a lifetime of identity conflict, I have come to accept that these are my people—by blood, even if not politically or spiritually. I have prayed with them, mourned with them, and celebrated their weddings. I share their rude tastes and humor, and I am marked by the same fundamentalist God-instilled self-loathing. No matter how much I may change or improve my condition, I cannot escape their pathos. I go forward, yet I remain. I wait anxiously and strive for change, for relief from what feels like an increased stifling of personal liberty, beauty, art, and self-realization in America. They wait in spooky calmness for Jesus.

Meanwhile, I am jolted by periodic reminders of fundamentalism's dark magical thinking. A couple of weeks ago, for example, I loaned my brother my old truck until he could get his engine rebuilt. A week later he returned the truck with sincere thanks, a smile, and an armload of frozen deer meat—most of it tenderloin, the stuff a hunter keeps for himself.

On the vent window of my old truck is a four-inch decal, a silhouette of two square dancers (my father-in-law, who gave me the truck, was a square dancer). When I climbed into the truck the next day, I noticed that the square dancers were covered over on both the inside and the outside with duct tape. I knew instantly why the decal was taped over. For spiritual protection. After all, we cannot be riding around in trucks with demonic emblems blasting out invisible rays of Satan's "Power of the Air," can we?

When I look at the fundamentalists I know personally, I see many kind, brave, and hardworking people, embodying all those things an American is supposed to be. But knowing what they used to be and what they have become, I see something else. I see that one of the most significant yet least understood political events in America is the conversion of millions of people from apolitical Christians into Christian political activists. Despite claims of independence, their churches have been deeply manipulated by their own power-hungry leadership and by the Republican Party, beginning in the Reagan years.

Future historians, however, may remember our political tumult as a lesser story in the end, because the current religious fervor may simply be the fourth in a series of Great Awakenings that have shaped America. None of the Awakenings involved the majority of Americans—most of them, like most of us today, were too busy with their lives to get involved in one of the great movements of their times. None of the Awakenings was about politics, but all of them had profound long-term political and social effects. The First Great Awakening occurred in the 1730s and 1740s, the Second in the 1820s and 1830s, the Third in the 1880s and early 1900s. The first three Awakenings were revivalist movements, not attempts to change government. It may well be that we are seeing the Fourth Awakening and that historians one day will document it as beginning in 1973 with the publication of R. J. Rushdoony's seminal *The Institutes of Biblical Law*. We will not know for some time; each previous Awakening took from twenty to thirty years to unfold and peak.

If this does prove to be the Fourth Awakening, then ours will have been the most radical of all. The First Awakening's James Davenport was seen as an insane extremist because he claimed to be able to distinguish the saved from the damned. Now all people are presumed to be damned until saved according to church specifications. We no longer even get a running start on the Devil! Davenport also believed in the banning and burning of books, even as Awakened preachers of the era declared the need for universal access to education because "at the foot of the cross the ground is level." If the preachers and participants of those earlier Awakenings saw Davenport as too extreme, then they would find Ted Haggard, Tim LaHaye, and many of today's leaders—men so powerful they advise the president—crazier than shithouse rats. Right up there with Grandpa Baldwin.

Fortune willing, this movement in American history—which is by no means over, since radical fundamentalism has managed to keep growing steadily in influence through both Democratic and Republican administrations—will be remembered as a dark time we managed to get through. Otherwise, one shudders to think of the outcome.

Backed by the faithful support of hardworking American Christians who seldom fully comprehend their leadership's agenda, zealous evangelical leaders will have no less than the "inevitable victory God has promised his new chosen people," according to the founding masters of the covert kingdom. Screw the Jews, they blew their chance. The 2008 elections, regardless of the outcome, will not change the fact that millions of Americans are under the spell of an extraordinarily dangerous mass psychosis. Maybe the philosopher Nietzsche was right: "One is not 'converted' to Christianity—one must first be sick enough for it."

Now I know I have cast a mighty wide net here, but only because these fish are many and slippery. No matter what one writes, fundamentalists come back with "Oh, but I am not that brand of fundamentalist." Then they launch into the tortuous doctrinal hairsplitting only they understand because nobody else in his or her right mind would bother reading such convoluted tomes. And by the time one finishes writing about them, they have shape-shifted into some slightly newer version of the same old game. Still, there is the fact that most ordinary fundamentalists don't like being directly associated with such extreme radicalism as Reconstructionism. Fundamentalists tell me, "No, I am not a Reconstructionist. Almost nobody is." Or "I am not a Premillennialist, I'm a Postmillennialist," or a "Midtribulationist" or . . . Whatever the arcane differentiation, they sure as hell share some of the same DNA.

I will spare you the agony of fundamentalist taxonomy and its mind-numbing explorations of theonomy and Erastianism. But if you are disposed toward self-punishment, you can take it upon yourself to learn the differences between Dominionism, Pretribulationism, Midtribulationism, Posttribulationism, Premillennialism, and Millennialism. You can spend ten years discussing them with ordinary fundamentalists of every stripe, and you still won't understand what has been going on with all those cults.

How did things arrive at this pass? Fred Clarkson, a New England Yankee with a streak of liberty a mile wide, has been thinking and writing about this longer than anybody I know. His book on the subject, *Eternal Hostility: The Struggle Between Theocracy and Democracys,* is a classic. He tells me that things got this far partly because of the energies of their leadership but more "because the rest of us were asleep at the wheel. They outsmarted us, they were organized, and they won fair and square." No demonic masterminds—or not as many or as masterly as we sometimes like to think, anyway. No handful of bogeymen or Dick Cheneys of fundamentalism we can point to as the root cause. There have been and still are plenty of slick leaders and operators, but in the end there is no quick television shot of *the* bad guy or guys.

The good news, Clarkson tells me, is that they came to power primarily through elections and can be dealt with in the same way: "Anyone who wishes to displace them needs to become more engaged in electoral politics than just watching it on television. You need to become engaged and bring your friends. And your family."

Just like the Christian right did.

The very nature of liberalism, with its emphasis on diversity and individuality, makes it hard to organize. The bigger problem, though, is that liberals, like most other Americans, have lost the skills of grassroots organization, not to mention the will. Clarkson observes, "Every good citizen should learn how to be a good activist—or a good candidate. Yes, it may mean making some choices, like less television and surfing the Internet. But that is how a constitutional democracy is organized. That's the way it works. If we abandon the playing field to the other side, they win by default." (If you are inspired to take immediate action, Wellstone Action at www.wellstoneaction.org has an excellent program and a manual. You can also find a very good reading list and discussion group at www.Talk2Action.org.)

Besides learning more about the religious right, we need to learn how to talk about them calmly and thoughtfully. "This is how good plans can be made," Clarkson tells me with Yankee practicality. The religious right these days claim that America was founded as a Christian nation, but "they seek to restore a theocratic order that never was, not since the ratification of the Constitution. The Framers of the Constitution overthrew 150 years of colonial theocracies and theocratic wannabes. And when it was accomplished, Benjamin Franklin said, 'You have a republic, if you can keep it.' So let's keep it."

Once we have learned the lay of the land, Clarkson adds, "We need to figure out who we can talk to and who we can't." When you get down to the guy in the church pew, he says, "You will find that most conservative evangelicals and fundamentalists do not want a theocracy and are not inclined to civil war here or in the Middle East. Their intellectual and political leaders may be, but most of the congregation just wants to pursue happiness in pretty much the same way as everyone else. It is time to get to know our neighbors." A couple of nights on the phone with Fred Clarkson convinced me he's right about that, even if he is a New England Yankee. Count me in.

But it sure as hell won't be easy, not down here where Satan's red-eyed demons howl like dogs and hover above us, suspended by mysterious aerial powers of the Devil himself.

6

The Ballad of Lynddie England

ONE FOOT IN ULSTER, THE OTHER IN IRAQ

When we look at the behavior of working-class American soldiers in places like Abu Ghraib, we cannot help but ask ourselves: How did they get so goddamned mean? And how did these Americans come to define our national ethos before the world in terms that are not entirely, or even mostly, true? Define us as a nation of gun fetishists (which we are not) worshipping a vengeful fundamentalist God (which most of us do not) and displaying a national arrogance and militarism that the world finds absolutely chilling (and they are, though so much of it is unthinking and unconscious).

Frankly, these have been major features of the American laboring class's ethos since the colonial era, when most men were entered on public records as "laborer" simply because there was so much backbreaking work to do in building the country—so much moving of logs, earth, and stone, so much clearing and digging and driving of ox wagons. As brutish labor coarsens the pleasures of its practitioners, common pastimes, particularly along the expanding edge of frontier America, included bear baiting, cockfights, eye-gouging contests, and other rough sport brought over from the Ulster Plantation by the group broadly known as the Scots Irish. No other group has affected our national ethos like the fierce, religious, war-loving Scots Irish, also known as the Ulster Scots and the Borderers—the people who are the subject of *Born Fighting: How the Scots-Irish Shaped America* by James Webb, the newly elected U.S. senator from Virginia.

From here in Winchester, Virginia, once the hub of colonial America's "Great Wagon Road," the largest crossroads of Scots-Irish history in America, we can easily see the Borderers' warring spirit and culture, which still flourishes in our churches, workplaces, voting booths, and bars. The mark of the Scots Irish on Winchester's people is clearly visible in the way we reject government while at the same time we are ultrapatriotic about "values" such as "defending our way of life," despite the fact that it has seldom if ever truly been threatened.

That strange mixture of working-class violence and Presbyterian piety that so mystifies secular minds has seldom been more virulent than it is at the beginning of our heavily armed entry into the twenty-first century—probably not since the Ulster Scots elected the first truly Scots-Irish president, Andrew Jackson, the Indian-killing, hog-and-hominy populist. Americans subsequently elected sixteen presidents in their likeness and a slew more who exemplified both the good and the bad in the Scots-Irish cultural soul. When I stand back and consider the pitiful specimens now getting elected by the current generation of my fellow beer-guzzling Borderer swine, Andrew Jackson doesn't look so bad. He may not have been Lincoln, but at least he had the guts to drink in public, butcher hogs in what is now the White House Rose Garden, and shoot at a couple of offensive upper-crust types. He was a rabid nationalist, a born warrior, and a fire-breathing American of the first order.

To this day what has been called "Jacksonian nationalism" remains the political foundation of those elements that might be called the Republican Party of Permanent War, the political wing of America's Corporate Military Industrial Complex. Lincoln predicted that the military industry would be the most fearful result of the Civil War. One hundred forty years later it has feasted and fattened itself through numerous American wars, actions, bombings, and military operations. Along the way it amassed enough wealth to literally purchase the government, systemically buy the political processes from within, and purge it of effete, softheaded Yankee liberalism. Fortunately for ambitious corporatists, there has always been a bad dog to sic on overly principled liberal snots who would argue that people should have more rights than property: the Ulster Scots and their descendants.

Sometimes when I hear the train go through Winchester, I am reminded that it goes to Fort Ashby, West Virginia, Lynndie England's hometown, on its way to Wheeling. We both grew up in about the same lower-class twentieth-century Scots-Irish circumstances. Life in a rundown rental was not much different here than in Lynndie's mobile home in Fort Ashby. It hasn't changed since George Washington built both the fort across the street from my house and the fort that gave Fort Ashby its name and protected Scots-Irish settlers there from the Indians.

When I walk the street where I grew up and when I look around, I see the likes of Lynndie everywhere—girls of the type I dated as a kid. Thanks to fast food (unavailable in my youth), they are fatter, but they are the same cigarette-smoking, in-your-face white girls I knew then, the tough daughters of the un-washed. Here in my old neighborhood, more than one-quarter of adults do not have a high school diploma, and there are lots of yellow ribbons in the windows, just like the ribbon on Lynndie England's family trailer, in honor of the women and men serving in Iraq or elsewhere on the far-flung perimeter of America's ex-panding empire of blood and commerce.

Whatever you think of the leash girl of Abu Ghraib, Lynndie England never had a chance. Abu Ghraib, or maybe something even worse (an RPG up the shorts, for instance), was always her destiny. Nearly half of the three thousand Americans killed thus far in Iraq are from small towns like hers, like mine—towns of fewer than forty thousand. Yet these towns make up only 25 per-cent of America's population. Most of the young soldiers were fleeing economically depressed places, or dead-end jobs like the one Lynndie had at the chicken-processing plant, though many deny it or do not even see it in their quick and ready patriotism and youthful blindness to the larger national scheme of things. These so-called volunteers are part of the nation's de facto draft—economic conscription. Money is always the best whip to use on the laboring classes. Thirteen hundred a month, a signing bonus, and free room and board sure beats the hell out of yank-ing guts through a chicken's ass.

And don't forget those big bucks for college later. Up to $65,000. Lynndie was supposedly going to college after her en-listment to become a "storm chaser," as in the Helen Hunt movie *Twister*. Perhaps many poor and working-class kids do go to col-lege on their military benefits. But I can count on one hand the number I know who did it. Let's be honest: Graduating from a small-town redneck high school not knowing where Alaska is on a map of the United States is not exactly the path to the bird-baths of Harvard Square. I suspect that down inside Lynndie knew her lot in life from the start; she wore combat boots and camo outfits to high school. She swore she loved it. If you are doomed to eat shit, you may as well bring your own fork. Such grim, unacknowledged resignation has long been a survival skill of Borderer people, an understanding that your life runs on a darker parallel track with success.

Since arriving in America during the first seventy-five years of the eighteenth century, Calvinist Ulster Scots have constituted a parallel culture to that of enlightened Yankee liberals. Scots-Irish Calvinist values all but guarantee anger and desire for vengeance against what is perceived as elite authority: college-educated secular people who run the schools, the media, and the courts and don't seem to mind if their preacher is a queer. One Calvinist premise has always dominated: The word of God supersedes any and all government authority. Period. That same flaming brand of Calvinism brought here by the Ulster Scots launched American Christian fundamentalism. Now it threatens to breach the separation of church and state. Worse yet, its most vehement elements push for a nuclear holy war.

Yes, push for a nuclear holy war. You may not meet them among your circle of friends, but there are millions of Americans who fiercely believe we should nuke North Korea and Iran, seize the Middle East's oil (KICK THEIR ASS AND TAKE THEIR GAS reads one bumper sticker). They believe the United States will conquer the entire world and convert it to American notions of democracy and fundamentalist Christian religion. Lately though, due to growing public distaste for their agenda and the Iraq War, they have abandoned terms such as *fundamentalist Christian* and *theocratic state* in favor of terms such as *Christian manliness.*

To understand how such ominous political ideations reveal themselves in this country, we must look back 450 years to a group of Celtic cattle thieves killing one another in the mud along Hadrian's Wall—the Borderers. Fanatically religious and war loving, these Scottish Protestants made their way first to Ireland as the "Ulster Scots," then to American shores during the early eighteenth century. These Scots-Irish Borderers brought cultural values that govern the political emotions of millions of Americans to this day. We have King James I of England to thank for this sordid state of affairs. My online friend Billmon, at www.billmon.com, who has made a study of the subject, says that more than any other person it was that sawed-off little Scot James who created the cultural psychosis that would spawn Jerry Falwell, Ian Paisley, George W. Bush, the Oklahoma bombings, *and* the red state–blue state electoral map.

That's a lot to pin on one head, even if it did wear a crown, Billmon admits. "But it's true," he insists. "Much of what made America America—and a lot of what the rest of the world has come to detest about us—can be traced back to this runty little Scotsman. There's enough irony there for a couple of Tom Stoppard plays, because King James, whose name became the brand for fundamentalist Christianity, also happened to be a notorious homosexual—one of the most enthusiastic practitioners in the long, proud history of British aristocratic buggery."

Like so many other English monarchs and prime ministers since his time, poor James was faced with trying to calm down some of the rioting and eye gouging at Ulster, Ireland, that ever-festering boil on the rump of British Protestantism. James's solution was to settle pockets of loyal Protestant Scots in the middle of Ulster's native Catholic population. The results were predictably nasty. Later, Ulster Scot Protestant loyalty was transferred to William of Orange, creating the Orangemen, the Irish equivalent of America's redneck fundamentalists—both troublesome to a free and orderly republic yet useful to the most malignant political elements.

Ultimately, a program of high prices, ruinous taxes, and destruction of employment drove the Ulster Scots to the more promising shores of the New World. Given the New World's primitive conditions and general lawlessness, they chose to revert back into the murderous Picts the British crown had come to know and love along Hadrian's Wall. Blessed with an abundance of guns, Indians for target practice, bountiful corn for homemade whiskey, and a hated government that insisted on taxing that whiskey, they forged a new and indelible element in American society: white trash, crackers, rednecks. People who had little use for government intrusions into such domestic aspects of life as moonshining, cockfighting, poaching, squatting on other people's land, and family feuds. These same people who had little use for an Injun and even less for a slave (their small homesteads in the hills were not conducive to the slave-based cotton and tobacco agriculture of their lowland "betters" living in the Tidewater plain of Virginia and the Deep South) set their seed to the winds. Their offspring spread westward, melding West and South together in a place called Texas. The violent frontier life suited them just fine, thank you. And thus we find them today, still armed and suspicious of government but also enraged about September 11—the best excuse to use firepower since the Alamo. Hell, since the Battle of Killiecrankie!

Only a year before September 11 they had come streaming out of every corner of the red states to crown George W. Bush as their own smirking William Wallace, leader of the 1297 rebellion against the English. Of the thirty Bush red states, twenty-three were among the top thirty Scots-Irish states. Of the top ten Scots-Irish states, Bush won all but one with an average vote share of more than 55 percent. Conversely, Bush won only two of the ten states with the lowest Scots-Irish population, North and South Dakota. Spiritually, philosophically, and politically, Borderer cultural influence still runs deep in America. So much so that, as David Hackett Fischer points out in his masterful synthesis of British-American folkways, *Albion's Seed,* Germans, Italians, Poles, and many other ethnic groups adopted the Scots-Irish values and mind-set as quintessentially American. Scots-Irish political culture in America holds and always has held many things that draw in other ethnic groups and contribute to the spreading of its ethos. It is populist and inclusive. The Scots Irish do not envy wealth in general and measure leaders by what they see as their personal strength, which usually comes down to whether they will fight for what they believe in, physically if necessary. And they are Christian, as were the majority of the Ellis Island wave of immigrants.

Another reason Borderer influence on America runs so deep is the Borderer affinity for nearly every kind of breedable human specimen; about one-third of Americans have a Borderer in the family. Yet until recently Scots-Irish culture has gone largely unexamined, maybe because it is so pervasive we take it for granted. The Scots Irish themselves know almost nothing of the history of their own culture. We are too busy living it and do not even identify ourselves as Scots Irish, which helps keep us invisible.

Liberal America in particular lives in thick-headed denial of what is obvious to nearly every working white person: A class conflict is being played out between the Scots-Irish culture and what James Webb rightly called America's "paternalistic Ivy League–centered, media-connected, politically correct power centers." Whether educated liberals believe this or not, it is true. Tens of millions of Scots Irish and thousands of Scots Irish–influenced communities believe it is true and vote as if it is true, and that makes it true.

Years ago, when Newt Gingrich became the first to describe the struggle in these terms, I winced because the truth of what he said was so obvious. Meanwhile, most Americans and the media in particular continue to use Borderer terms and values, such as "fierce, liberty loving," "individualistic," "freely religious," and "fighting to defend our way of life," to describe America and Americans. Unfortunately, the neoconservative takeover of American politics intensified this slogan-as-political-awareness approach, thereby supercharging the old familiar themes: fanatical religiosity, bellicose piety, and, in a new twist, the high-tech fist of Jesus smiting godless heathen in the name of a crude oil-stained flag.

Like it or not, most of what the world has traditionally seen as American-style democracy originates somewhere within these Christian Borderer precepts, especially the idea of a broad, shared prosperity. Scots-Irish immigrants in the New World sent home glowing reports and passage money to their relatives in Ulster. Archbishop Hugh Boulter of Armagh, in a letter to Lord New-castle in July 1728, complained of letters inviting fellow Irish to "transport themselves thither, and promising them liberty and ease as the reward of their honest industry, with a prospect of transmitting their acquisitions and privileges safe to their pos-terity, without the imposition of growing rents and other heavy burdens." If that isn't the consummate expression of the Ameri-can Dream, at least as it is perceived by most working stiffs and new immigrants, I don't know what is.

Along with the concept of the American Dream runs the no-tion that every man and woman is entitled to an opinion and to one vote, no matter how ridiculous that opinion might be or how uninformed the vote. It could be that the Borderer Presbyterian tradition of "stand up and say your rightful piece" contributed to the American notion that our gut-level but uninformed opinions are some sort of unvarnished foundational political truths. I have been told this is because we redneck working-class Scots Irish suffer from what psychiatrists call "no insight." Consequently, we will never agree with anyone from outside our zone of igno-rance because our belligerent Borderer pride insists on the right to be dangerously wrong about everything while telling those who are more educated to "Bite my ass!" After a night of political discussion at Royal Lunch, a British relative, a distant continen-tal member of the Bageant clan, called our gang of locals "the most intellectually squalid people I have ever met"—and he had chewed qat with Ugandan strongman Idi Amin's bodyguards.

Lynndie Rana England was born in 1982. I have a son her age. Like my son, she graduated high school in 2001. Folks in Fort Ashby say she did well in school, which is no great achievement in these places where the academic bar is set so damned low it is buried in the ground in hopes that any student who bothers to attend school will meander across it. After graduating, true to local form, she got married at age nineteen to James Fike, a nice local kid, a grocery stock boy. I'm sure she married mostly out of small-town boredom. I got married that way once, though I've got sense enough now to be positively embarrassed to tell you how young I actually was.

Anyway, Lynndie was married to James Fike when she enlisted in 2003. However, enlistment led to a "relationship" with a fellow reserve unit member at Abu Ghraib named Charles Graner, and pregnancy at age twenty-one. By the end of 2003 came the standard low-rent divorce papers exchange between Fike and England. This was four months before the Abu Ghraib scandal broke, but already there were clues. While home on leave, Lynndie told her divorce lawyer that "bad things" were going on at Abu Ghraib. She said prisoners were being forced to exercise until they dropped from exhaustion and to wear women's underwear on their heads. She said lots of OGAs (other government agencies) were involved. Anyone who was ever in the military knows that "other government agencies" means the CIA. You don't fuck with or question the CIA. Lynndie said,

"They said, 'Good job. Keep it up.'" She thought it was weird, but she kept it up.

Lynndie has given only one interview, and a revealing one at that, to Tara McKelvey of *Marie Claire* magazine. Though under the close supervision of her lawyer, she alluded to hangings conducted in doorways at Abu Ghraib and to the sodomizing of young Iraqi boys by one of the contractors. But her overarching story is a common and plausible one to be found in any trailer court or blue-collar burg in America—falling for the wrong guy for the wrong reasons in the wrong place.

Lynndie was at Abu Ghraib during a particularly bad time. Prisoners tried to riot. Enemy mortars pounded the place at night, and the air was choked with concrete dust. Snipers picked away at guards during the day. There was terror inside, terror outside. Her former commander, Brigadier General Janis Karpinski, told McKelvey that "in situations like Iraq, the first thing some young female soldiers look for is a protector—a senior male" (all of which is oddly reminiscent of the domestic prison environment). "Enter Charles Graner," said Karpinski. "He's much older, and he's full of himself. He's just got that kind of personality. . . . She was blown away."

Spc. Charles A. Graner Jr. is now pulling ten years. So we must presume that the former prison guard who loved taking close-ups of blow jobs in storage rooms, who loved anal sex with Lynndie, often with her giving the thumbs-up gesture that would become infamous, has hung up his camera for most of the next decade. Still, there's that question: Why did she do those things?

"I just wanted to make him happy," she told her lawyer, Roy Hardy. "I didn't want him to take the pictures," she told McKelvey, "but he took pictures of everything. . . . He kept a camera in his cargo pocket. He was always taking his camera out."

Graner had his camera ready on the night he led a mentally ill prisoner nicknamed Gus—who, according to trial records, smeared feces on his body and threatened to kill the guards—out of his cell with a tie-down strap around his neck. He handed it to Lynndie so he could take a picture. One more time Lynndie helped Graner feel good. Graner snapped the picture and e-mailed it to his family in Pennsylvania. "Look what I made Lynndie do," he wrote.

Lynndie England is now serving out a thirty-six-month sentence in the Naval Consolidated Brig Miramar in San Diego. She no longer thinks much about chasing tornadoes like Helen Hunt. She was up for parole in the fall of 2006. No one believed she would get it, and they were right. So England is taking computer and electronic equipment repair classes. It's not storm chasing, but at least she will be employable when she gets out.

If we Borderer spawn seem inured to squalid and uncomfortable living in the American empire's bleakest corners, then we "git it honest" as they say around here. The homeland of the original Borderers was a bleak and squalid place, denuded of forests and incapable of growing enough food to support its inhabitants, much less enough to sell at market. The natives survived by and gloried in "reiving," or cattle rustling. It was a land of famine and overpopulation, the only constant being warfare between England and Scotland along the shifting border. Rooted in centuries of national fighting—and, during rare periods of peace, in interclan warfare—the Borderers maintained their fierce ways, clan loyalties, and holdings. The right to hold any turf they occupied was established by their ability to defend it. Holding such miserable land was a worthwhile effort to the extent that it provided enough space so clans could be together with enough strength in numbers to—what else?—defend the miserable land, a full-time occupation that came to define the culture. This vicious, nearly pointless cycle manifests itself today in the American belief that you can retain only that for which you are willing to fight, be it a grand notion like democracy or a humble thing like one's cabin.

Speaking of cabins, given the unceasing looting, burning, and moving, the Borderers built impermanent earth and log dwellings called "cabbins." Within their smoky confines they lived a quick-tempered, hard-drinking, volatile lifestyle, one that anthropologists say is still evident in some American trailer courts today. So the next time you see one of us drunkenly kicking in a neighbor's car door in a trailer court parking lot at 1 a.m., try to remember: That's not a brawl you're witnessing, it's cultural diversity.

The Borderers embraced the most fanatical form of Calvinism. In justifiable reaction to the corrupt Roman Catholic church of their time, the Johns—Knox and Calvin—established the democratic organization of the Presbyterian church, with Jesus Christ as the church's only primate. After failing in efforts to make Scotland's government a theocracy, Presbyterian Scots settled for the next worst thing—putting Christ as the arbiter of all civil government. They decreed that any civil government was only as legitimate as it was biblical, and they reserved the right to resist civil government if it did not meet those standards. As theological ideas go, John Calvin had slammed one out of the park.

Halfway around the world and across four centuries, Calvin is the undisputed father of American Christian fundamentalism, which still clings to those same conclusions about God and government. His American Borderer descendants are busily dismantling the mainspring of their hated government, the U.S. Constitution, and for the past thirty years "Dominionist" fundamentalists have worked politically to replace it with "Biblical Law" according to their own interpretation. So far it is about the only thing they have not succeeded in doing. In any case, Calvin would jump out of that grave and demand a high five if he knew the effect his movement has had on the world's most powerful empire.

Looking back, it is hard to believe such a motley swarm of border Celts as arrived in America could accomplish all that. They certainly appeared unlikely candidates when they began migrating here during the first seventy-five years of the eighteenth century, quite often as ship's ballast. That's right. A useful purpose had been found for even the drunkest Borderer, one that required absolutely no skill whatsoever. There was much empty space, and therefore too much buoyancy, in returning colonial ships that had carried American flaxseed to Ulster's linen mills. What could be better on the nearly empty return voyage than a weighty cargo, no matter how drunk and unsavory, a cargo that could load and unload itself and was actually willing to pay to serve as ballast? So unsavory were Borderer habits that upon arrival in America even fellow Calvinists, the New England Puritans, would not accept them. They were less than enamored with the Borderers' practice of drinking in church and with their low hygienic standards.

There was an even more fundamental difference between the Borderers and the Puritan followers of Cotton Mather's brand of Calvinism. Unlike the Puritans, the Borderers, though religious, did not emigrate for religious reasons. They did not come to these shores seeking democracy or an end to royalty. They came because rent and taxes were too high and work was too scarce in Ulster. The Ulster Scots were one of the most exploited groups of their time, racked and wrenched by landowning squires for every penny and ounce of labor that could be extracted. They were treated like a disposable labor force, every individual pitted against everyone else for survival in a successful business model emulated by American business today. So it is understandable that gratitude was rare among these Scots. Before long, Scot Presbyterian ministers angered the English colonial establishment in America as they rabble-roused their poor scratching, ignorant congregations by "bellowing from their pulpits against ye Landlords and ye Clargey, calling them Rackers of Rents and Scruers of Tythes."

In a couple of decades the Borderers found themselves once more on a border—the border of Western civilization along the frontiers of Pennsylvania. True to form, they were exactly where they were not supposed to be: tilling soil and killing Indians west of the Allegheny Mountains in defiance of King George II's prohibition. In the long run, however, these hard-fighting fanatics turned out to be useful to aristocrats eager to develop their vast land grants in the colonies. For example, from the 1730s onward, the Virginia planter elite sought to populate the Blue Ridge Mountains as a barrier between the Indians and their lowland slave plantations and sold the Shenandoah Valley to those willing to settle there. Elites such as Thomas Lord Fairfax and the

Byrd and the Beverly families of Virginia brought in Borderers, along with sturdy Pennsylvania Germans. The Borderers seemed more than willing to keep the Indians, and later the French, killed back behind a line along the Alleghenies, and Virginia's leading families made fortunes that stand today from the land sales, especially sales to German settlers. From the beginning, Virginia was about land speculation and development, and today we find the descendants of those early elites selling yet again this valley's fields and woods to those purchasing their way deeper and deeper into the suburban sprawl.

The Borderers, however, squatted on nearly as much as they purchased, or they shot at rent collectors. The young officer George Washington, while building Winchester's French and Indian War frontier defenses at Fort Loudoun, called our town one of the most ignorant, mean-spirited, and predatory places in all the colonies, a tradition we have thus far managed to maintain. Washington disliked the locals. The locals disliked him in return for closing so many of the taverns that preyed upon his soldiers. That did not keep Washington from marching said uncouth souls—my ancestors among them—into the Alleghenies to "take a pull," as an early account puts it, at the menacing French and the murderous feathered heathen.

Not too many years later, when the elitist, land-speculating Washington entered politics, he had barrels of rum rolled out on our main street, and the same unwashed and mean-spirited Winchesterians elected him to his first public office, member of the Virginia House of Burgesses. Which goes to show that no political idea or personage is so unpalatable to us that it cannot be washed down with a drink or otherwise made acceptable through God rhetoric and some patriotic bloody-shirt waving. It still works. Repeated showings of Twin Towers footage and beheadings via the Internet are the kind of bloody shirt an America steeped in Borderer culture can grasp.

In the ensuing 260 years, working-class products of Borderer culture, particularly in the South, have remained useful to the rich and the politically ambitious, including most of the same rich old-line families locally: the Byrds, Lees, Carters, and Glasses. During the Civil War, although we were too poor to piss straight, we nevertheless died in the hundreds of thousands to protect slavery on behalf of the elite plantation owners (40 percent of all wealth in the South was in the form of slaves held by the elite). Later, during the Jim Crow era, we Virginia Borderers were indispensable to the Harry Flood Byrd political machine in helping to "keep the niggers down," as they used to say. In Virginia we shut down the state's public schools and sent our kids to school in the Methodist and Pentecostal and Baptist church basements during Harry Flood Byrd's "massive resistance" to the school integration campaign. And to this day we can be counted on for bellicose objection to such government oppression as health care for the poor, equitable taxation of the rich (no kind of tax can be good to a Borderer), fair labor practices, seat belts, and environmental laws.

Most of the early Borderer immigrants first went to Pennsylvania. From there they spread north and south, and later west, and assimilated into the cultures they found. Those who went south identified with the South during the Civil War. Those who went north identified with the North, and so on, as they spread their strain throughout the nation. And what a strain! Every damned one of them was part wampus cat, "part Cherokee," ever malleable by the swells, and presently more than happy to give any deserving Muslim a .45-caliber ticket to paradise. Ready to ship out for the next holy war on any shore that flies a heathen banner. To our minds, what could possibly be wrong with making the world heel to an empire piloted by Calvin's ghost and anointed by God? Love us or hate us, we are nevertheless the same pathos-ridden, stubborn, God-obsessed folks who gave you Johnny Cash, Andrew Jackson, Ma Barker, Ronald Reagan, Mark Twain, country music, NASCAR, Edgar Allan Poe, John Hancock, and Bill Clinton.

But a good blood-rousing war is where we truly shine—where God, patriotism, glory, and mayhem come together in the Borderer scheme of things. America's discontent with the Iraq War will eventually shut it down, as did discontent with the Vietnam War. But we will always be sucker bait for the next war until the system that sustains ignorance-as-patriotism and militant religiosity ends. I receive e-mails from Iraq, compliments of a born-again coworker, which I in turn forward to progressive friends in liberal cities, who write them off as the screeds of religious nut jobs. But there are millions of said nut jobs who exercise their right to vote. Here is an excerpt from one such e-mail from a U.S. government–designated "embedded reporter" who writes for the church newsletter of an Arlington, Virginia, Assembly of God congregation. The owner of a small bakery shop, one of hundreds of rabid evangelists sent to Iraq over the past three years along with legitimate journalists, he has been deemed a news reporter by the Bush administration.

> Blessings from the land of Babylon!
>
> . . . It makes me so angry that these quiet warriors receive no appreciation from the media. . . . The media is a pack of lying, deceiving whores who will go to any length to defeat George Bush and the righteousness of this cause to set these helpless people free from antichrist spirit through Saddam and his wicked sons, Uday and Usay. . . . There are two lords, we follow one or the other. There is JESUS or there is the devil. . . . Call those liberal lying rags like the Washington Post, L.A. Times, N.Y. Times, CBS and the CNN [communist news network] and voice your disapproval of their lying. . . . As the song goes "do you know JESUS and does HE know you."
>
> GOD BLESS
Michael

And they say we do not engage in holy wars.

The Scots-Irish working-class culture's take on the world is that it was always a tough place and is getting tougher. For the guy or gal who installs your phone line or stocks the produce shelves at your upscale grocery store, it often comes down to this: Drink, pray, fight, and fuck. Kill the bad guys. He or she might be born-again and therefore not a drinker, but the net conservative belief is the same. "Life ain't really that complicated, folks. Quit whining. Kill the bastards if that's what it takes. Or even if it doesn't. It'll make 'em think."

* * *

We rural and small-town mutt people seem by an early age to have a special capacity for cruelty. For instance, as a child did you ever put a firecracker up a toad's ass and light it? George W. Bush and I have that in common. As nonwhites the world round understand, white people can be mean, especially if they feel threatened—and they feel threatened about everything these days. But when you provide certain species of white mutt people with the right incentives, such as approval from God and government, you get things like lynchings, Fallujah, the Birmingham bombers. You get Abu Ghraib.

Even as this is being written, we may safely assume that some of my tribe are stifling the screams of captives in America's secret "black site" prisons across the planet. On a more mundane scale, they might be (as seen in CBS footage) kicking and stomping hundreds of chickens to death every day at the Pilgrim's Pride plant in Moorefield, West Virginia, not too far from where I am writing, and where Lynndie once worked. Or consider the image of Matthew Shepard's body twisted on that Wyoming fence. That too is our handiwork. We, the mutt-faced working-class sons and daughters of the Scots-Irish republic, born to kick your chicken breast meat to death for you in the darkest, most dismal corners of our great land, born to kill and be killed in stock-car races, in drunken domestic rows, and of course in the desert dusty back streets at the edges of the empire.

Middle-class urban liberals may never claim us as brothers, much less as willing servants, but as they say in prison, we are your meat. We do your bidding. Liberals' refusal to admit that we do your dirty work for you, not to mention international smack-downs and muggings for the Republic—from which you benefit more materially than we ever will—makes it no less true.

Literally from birth, we get plenty of conditioning to kill those "gooks" and "sand monkeys" and whoever else needs a lesson at any particular moment in history according to our leadership. Like most cracker kids in my generation, from the time I could walk I played games in which I pretended to kill Japanese, Indians, Germans, Koreans, Zulus (as seen in the movies *Zulu* and *Uhuru!*), variously playing the role of U.S. cavalry, Vikings à la Kirk Douglas, World War II GIs, colonial soldiers, and of course Confederate soldiers. As little white cracklets we played with plastic army men that we tortured with flame, firecracker, burning rivulets of gasoline, kerosene, lighter fluid, and, if atomic bombing was called for, M80s and ash cans. We went to sleep dreaming of the screams of the evil brutes we had smitten that day, all those slant-eyed and swasticated enemies of democracy and our way of life.

Later, as post-cracklets in high school, we rode around in cars looking to fight anyone who was different, be they black, brown, or simply from another school or county. As young men we brawled at dances and parties or simply while staring at one another bored and drunk. We bashed each other over women, less-than-weight bags of dope, money owed, and alleged insults to honor, wife, mother, or model of car—Ford versus Chevy—in other words, all of white trash culture's noblest causes. With the fighting tradition of Scots Irish behind us, we smash each other up ceaselessly in trailer court and tavern, night and day, in rain and summer heat, until finally we reach our midfifties and lose our enthusiasm (not to mention stamina) for that most vener-ated of Borderer sports.

Said meanness is polished to a high gloss of murderous piety most useful to the military establishment. Thus, by the time we are of military age (which is about twelve), we are ca-pable of doing a Lynndie England on any type of human being unfamiliar to us. Sent to Iraq or Afghanistan, most of us, given the nod and enough stress, seem capable of torturing "the other" as mindlessly as a cat plays with a mouse. That we can do it so readily and without remorse is one of the darkest secrets under-lying the "heroes" mythology the culture machine is so fervently ginning up about the series of wars now unfolding. When one of us is killed by a rooftop sniper in Baghdad, we weep and sweat, banding closer together as Borderer brothers in the ancient oath of ultimate fealty and courage.

It's been that way all my life, and I doubt it will end until the American empire declines and the reigning Caesar, Republi-can or Democrat, no longer needs the mutt people. Pure mean-ness is highly valued in Caesar's legions. Lots of Americans don't seem to mind having a pack of young Scots-Irish American pit bulls savage some fly-blown desert nation, or run loose in the White House for that matter, so long as they are *our* pit bulls pro-tecting Wall Street and the 401(k)s of the middle class.

The problem is this: Pit bulls always escalate the fight and keep at it until the last dog is dead, leaving the gentler breeds to clean up the blood spilled.

Sitting on her cot in her military prison cell, Lynndie En-gland is no longer the waif in the Abu Ghraib photos. She smells like soap, writes Tara McKelvey. "She rubs her hands constantly, and her cuticles are raw and bleeding. Her hair is pulled back in four tortoiseshell clips, and it's streaked with premature gray," McKelvey reports. She has had visitors only once, and then only because McKelvey provided the opportunity to her mother, her sister Jesse, and her baby, Carter, son of Charles Graner Jr., the soldier who shot the pictures that outraged the world.

Even before Graner's pictures were made public, they seem to have been more public at the prison than the brass has ever admitted. The photograph of the human pyramid was used as a screen saver, according to military investigators. That it would seem safe to do such a thing in the usually ultrastrict military environment says a great deal about the attitudes of the higher-ups at Abu. You don't take chances in a terror-filled military prison just for laughs.

But maybe you do for love. Or to feel a sense of belonging. The girl from the trailer park next to the roadside beer joint at Fort Ashby, West Virginia, did. Monster of Abu or not, she once hung out with other kids at Evan's Dairy Dip and once was a member of the Future Farmers of America. No one in her family ever earned a college degree. She joined the army because she wanted the money for college. She quit her job at the infamous Pilgrim's Pride chicken plant because "people were doing bad things. Management didn't care." Just like the people at Abu Ghraib were doing bad things. Management didn't care there either.

So she waits out her sentence as a high-profile prisoner. Unlike other inmates, she isn't allowed to take the flag down at day's end. After all, someone might snap another picture of her. And our empire definitely doesn't need any more shots of little Scots-Irish girls too damned eager to please.

7

An Authorized Place to Die

THE AMERICAN HEALTH CARE SYSTEM ON
LIFE SUPPORT

Not everyone around here is concerned with the fate of our Constitution, nor is everyone a born-again Christian. Our favorite karaoke singer, Dottie, patriotic soul that she is, never gives the Constitution a thought, and she surely hasn't spent enough time on a church pew to keep the dust off.

But the Devil got her anyway, and now she is living in Romney, West Virginia, one of hell's halfway houses, where the Devil stashes lost souls until he can further deal with them. Having finally gotten her Social Security Disability Insurance approved, Dot lives in a ten-unit "assisted living facility." In true Dottie fashion, she's making the best of it, even enjoying it, mostly because at last she has dependable medical care and can be sure that she will not be kicked out of her home as she sucks on her oxygen bottle twenty-four hours a day and talks to her bird, Buddy. Between trips to the hospital, she also pushes on with her karaoke career.

She applied for the facility ages ago without telling her husband. "I was planning to divorce the slug bastard anyway. I found out he's had a little gal on the side for years. I'm back here in Romney. Actually, it's where I grew up."

Even if she were not from Romney, it is not surprising that

she'd end up here or someplace like it, an out-of-sight place where many working folks in our town find themselves when they're too old and worn-out to work anymore. Though towns like these are typical of heartland America, we sophisticates here in Winchester, the buckle of the butter-and-egg belt, grew up seeing Romney as the dismal end of the earth, our own little Third World neighbor just over the state line. Yes, in the great scheme of the new globalized America, it is our own little Bangladeshi village, providing local industry with cheap hillbilly labor. There's almost no work in Romney itself, or in the next closest town, Fort Ashby, but it is a place to bunk when residents are not working.

On the other hand, some folks look at Romney as offering easy, affordable living. Blessed with four "dollar stores," it is a place where for $359 you can rent your own house—$250 if you aren't choosy and scratch around hard enough—and comfortably enjoy the slow-paced life of killing yourself by alcohol and tobacco night after night on a minimum wage. It's a matter of perspective.

The population of Romney is 1,975 souls. Ninety-seven percent of all the hides in town are whiter than the belly of a fish. There are eight Mexicans and ten Asian Indians, nearly all of whom are family members of Indian doctors practicing there. More than a third of the population is over retirement age, and a lot of the rest are challenged by the same ignorant redneck background I come from. White as this place is, its people suffer from most of the same problems as urban blacks. They have a high incarceration rate and a low graduation rate, and they bear a good number of children out of wedlock. It's the kind of place where, as one young woman put it, "They'll call you a snob for being too good to have a boyfriend in jail." When it comes to medical care, Romney has a hospital after a fashion (Hampshire Memorial), and a few doctors. Which brings us to the subject of Dottie and doctors and the way the working poor are discarded when they can no longer work.

It is Saturday and Dottie is yakking with me on the phone while my wife rolls the old evil eye at me for typing with a drink in my hand at 11:30 in the morning. Meanwhile, Dottie angles for a ride to the crafts fair over in Kaiser. She's in a wheelchair when she goes out now, and she needs someone to push her. One more drink and the Bageant household may get hot enough that I will be forced to give Dottie that ride to Kaiser. I may find myself pushing that wheelchair among the crocheted bears, painted gourds, and red, white, and blue hillbilly dream catchers just to get out of here.

An hour later I am at Dot's, watching her cockatiel Buddy walk over, under, and around the oxygen tube and across the top of her head as she talks. "People tell me I should wean myself off this oxygen," she says. "I tell 'em, 'Put a plastic bag over your own head and wean yourself.'"

Dottie is doping out the Romney medical establishment for me: "These Indians or Pakis or whatever they are run the hospital like it was a cheap motel. The place is dirty." In her experience, they don't give out pain medication when they're supposed to. I have to admit that that's a pretty good trick in a place where most of your patients are tough rednecks who think biting down on a lead bullet during major surgery constitutes pain relief.

"Anyhow," Dot sighs, "I looked our hospital up at www .healthgrades.com. Cost me seven dollars." (Dottie is unusual for her age and class in that she has fully embraced the Internet, as a result of her immobility. Consequently, she has learned how to gain the information she needs, not to mention increased her vocabulary by leaps and bounds.) "I learned that damned towelhead doctor of mine has only four years of college someplace in South America."

No doubt you are wincing at the racist term *towelhead.* But people do talk that way, and if we use it as an excuse not to listen, we rule out listening to half of America. And besides, bad language aside, Second and Third World hack doctors *do* come to the United States and practice medicine in places like Romney, West Virginia, and Winchester, Virginia. I dare any reader in high dudgeon to come on down here and let one of these doctors treat you for your next serious illness.

Dottie continues: "Honest to damned, I think these doctors are here to take out the old and crippled people in this country. Kill 'em off in out-of-the-way places where the public can't see. They treat all of us like they expect us to die and like they expect to make money on us right up to the last minute."

Dottie speaks from experience. She used to work at the Winchester hospital, where she often wheeled dying patients in their eighties and nineties to get one last expensive scan before they died. Once she had to take along a nurse, who gave a poor old bastard CPR three times on the way to get a final billable CAT scan out of his insurance. He died minutes later.

Dottie's eighty-eight-year-old mother is in the nursing home section of the hospital, which occupies most of the building. Her husband died of black lung, and she has it too, along with several other diseases, including dementia (the quick-and-dirty diagnosis of which offers an easy route through the paperwork of admission). Many miners' wives contract black lung from doing their husband's laundry, riding in his vehicle, and living in a black lung town. For years Dot's mother's expenses were paid by a coal miners' benefits fund. But Mom recently reached the fund's stated limit, so Medicare—which pays for less than the miners' fund—has taken over.

Like anyone who actually looks out for a parent in these low-rent nursing facilities, Dottie is constantly monitoring her mother's care. "He never saw her at all until I jumped his ass about it," she says.

Working-class families are often so respectful or wary of professionals they never challenge them. Not Dottie. "Looky here, Doc," Dottie told the doctor when he cited her mother's dementia as a reason she might not have remembered his visits, "don't run that on me. I'm not afraid of you. My mother can remember the lyrics to every damned song she ever sang and can hold an intelligent conversation with anyone. She can beat anybody in here at cards and can name all her grandkids and their birthdays! She got in here because she broke a hip, that's all."

"Well, I saw your mother in the dining room when I went through last week. She looked just fine to me."

"In the dining room? If you took the trouble to examine her you'd know she may have pneumonia, and she sure as hell has a very painful rotator cuff."

"What are you saying? That I bill for services I am not rendering? Those are serious charges," he says. The doctor walks over to Dottie's mom's bed, asks the old woman how she feels, then walks on down the hall.

A word like *charges* carries a lot of weight with less educated working folks. Around here, anything that sounds vaguely legal scares most working people to death because they know that even saying hello to a lawyer costs more money than they have. Wealthy people have lawyers for payback. Poor people have them for DUIs.

In America your economic status pretty much determines your social status. A dentist's wife is treated differently than her nanny. People like Dot are treated as inconsequential, matter-of-factly insulted by doctors, lawyers, and administrators who might not even realize they are doing it. If I dress down and drop a few consonants, the same thing happens to me. All of this is dictated, of course, by access to higher education, which is mostly determined by economic status.

Dottie's encounter with her mother's doctor made me think of my own mother, living in a Winchester nursing home that echoes with moans of "Heeeelp me" day and night. Like every other person with a parent in that nursing home, I make average money, work fifty-five hours a week counting the commute, have a spouse with two part-time jobs of her own, and a house that is old and all stairs. We all feel guilty that we cannot care for our parents at home in the way that they cared for theirs, and our parents cannot understand why we are barely getting by with two people working a total of 118 hours a week. How is one of us supposed to stay home and enjoy this wonderful new jobless economy with our elderly parents knitting by the fireside? It cracks us up to hear the well-off baby boomers on NPR talking about "selecting the right care facility for elderly parents." Our family's choice, like Dot's, was either the Hallmont in Winchester, which smells like shit and Pine-Sol, or the one in Romney, which smells like shit and piss. We chose the closer one, and I push Mom around in her wheelchair while she puffs Camel filters. Like Dot's mom, mine seldom sees a doctor unless something goes very wrong.

Like a slumlord's rentals, such nursing homes are merely spaces that allow the proprietors, doctors, and health administrators to generate money for themselves through our government's approach to care. Most, if not all, of the money at these middle-grade establishments now comes from the government in the form of Medicaid and Medicare payments for services— everything from medical procedures to toenail clipping and special diets. The dependency is greater in rural and working-class urban areas, less in affluent places, many of which manage to receive a disproportionately high share of government reimbursements. Medicaid was designed during the sixties to meet the needs of Americans under age sixty-five without health insurance, after which age Medicare would kick in protecting all Americans over sixty-five. But the new jobless economy that drove Wall Street to new heights somehow left us with 45 million uninsured Americans, pushing Medicaid enrollment from 33 million to 56 million between 2001 and 2005 alone. This was accompanied by the nearly complete destruction of the public hospital system and health clinics by HMOs and Bush administration funding cuts, and by the rise of false nonprofit hospital networks. Meanwhile, although Medicare and Medicaid serve some 87 million people one way or another, a 2007 budget proposal calls for a $10.6 billion slash in funding for Medicaid and Medicare in order to preserve their "solvency." True, these programs consumed $417 billion of the nation's $2.338 trillion 2006 budget. But Pentagon programs consumed $419 billion, yet nobody seems to be inquiring about the Pentagon's solvency.

When it comes to on-the-ground delivery of nursing care services, it doesn't matter to the government that many staff members are functionally illiterate. All that matters is that a nursing home is an authorized place in which people can die. A thirty-four-bed facility like Romney's Hampshire Memorial can easily pull in $2 million or $3 million a year. That may not sound like much these days, but if a business manager skins the cat right, it provides a good living for the doctors and others who work there.

"Ya know, I used to be so proud of the hospital," Dottie recalls. "I grew up here and I can remember back in 1959 when it opened. I was its fourth patient. And later I had three of my kids here. Oh, this hospital was the most wonderful thing! It was so bright and spotless. People got X-rays who had never had them before. Old farmers got blood tests and tetanus shots for the first time in their lives. We had two doctors, Dr. Brown and Dr. Brown, brothers. They raised their kids here. They knew as much medicine as any doctor did in those days. Now half the hospital has been converted to a profitable shithouse that passes for a nursing home. Everybody avoids coming here unless it is life and death. And sometimes not even then."

The hospital portion of the building remains, but mostly as an anteroom on the way into the long-term care center. There is no receptionist to be seen. Finally, when I caught an orderly passing through, I asked him a couple of questions about the hospital.

"Oh no, we don't deliver babies or offer medical services," said the orderly. "People go to Winchester or Cumberland, Maryland, for that. But if somebody came in from a car crash, we'd take care of them." *Clinic* might be the best word to describe the place. So if Dottie's heart fails, she will be hauled thirty-seven miles to the Winchester Medical Center in an ambulance tended by a couple of volunteers.

The little hospital of Dottie's fond memories, the one that delivered the town's babies and later took out their appendixes, was not seized away by unscrupulous Hindu doctors. The life was sucked out of it by the Winchester Medical Center and other hospitals in the region, leaving Romneyites like Dottie to squint at its desanguinated carcass much the same way desert residents ponder those mysterious cattle mutilations. It was another victim of America's vast network of nonprofit hospital chains.

Only 16 percent of American hospitals are for-profit. About 80 percent of American hospital beds are owned by nonprofit hospitals, which wield tremendous power in the market. (These interesting facts and many others can be found in Maggie Mahar's excellent book, *Money-Driven Medicine: The Real Reason Health Care Costs So Much*.) How did nonprofits become so dominant? Over the past twenty-five years a boatload of America's for-profit hospitals migrated to nonprofit status because it is more profitable. They make billions of dollars without doing many of the things the public associates with nonprofit work. As best I can tell, they are in the real estate and tax escape business.

Here's how it works: You place an untaxable hospital in a desirable location, smack in the middle of a population that is growing and becoming more affluent, such as booming Frederick County, Virginia, in which our old town of Winchester is situated. Because the hospital is nonprofit, it is exempt from state and local property taxes. So while you make plenty of money selling medical services, the rising real estate values increase your capital assets steadily. But best of all, nonprofit hospitals are exempt from corporate income taxes, and that exemption is especially valuable to hospitals located in the most affluent areas because their income is so high and their property is worth so much. At the same time, these hospitals draw more well-insured patients and see fewer uninsured patients.

Such keen strategizing soon leaves you sitting on a pile of cash, yet you cannot take a profit. Naturally, your first thought is to expand. So you plow that money into taking market share away from neighboring hospitals, sucking up even more medical dollars and growing into a regional medical center, leaving small hospitals in small communities like Romney on life support.

As for providing health care to indigent patients, these hospitals may be tax-exempt nonprofits, but they are by no means charity hospitals, and their administrators will be the first to admit it. Like for-profit hospitals, they do not locate in places where their customers cannot pay for service. Luckily for them, they can legally preserve their tax-exempt status by treating only a handful of charity patients each year, so long as they offer things like diabetic support groups and other low-cost public information services. A wellness center is another way for a nonprofit hospital to discharge its obligations to the poor. So if a poor diabetic person manages to survive insulin shock and lives to make the payments on the credit card he used for that emergency room visit, he is welcome to join a hundred others like him down at the community center for a wellness talk and a free brochure paid for by a leading pharmaceutical company.

If he lives in Winchester, or cares to drive down from Romney, he might press his nose against the window of our new $17 million, 55,000- to 60,000-square-foot exercise and wellness center, complete with four-lane pool and running track, soon to be located on the campus of the massive Winchester Medical Center, which is owned by the nonprofit chain Valley Health. With $170 million parked in cash and reserves, what else is there to do but put Nautilus and Gold's Gym out of business? Parent company Valley Health projects that the wellness center business will be paid for after its second year (no debt service when you've got $170 million in loose change) and after the third year "will throw off a $1.3 million cash flow." Dena Kent, executive director of wellness for the outfit, says it's all part of their outreach. Valley Health may be reaching out, but when the hand draws back, your wallet is $800 a year lighter. (That's a typical membership fee.)

Simple common sense should tell us that this money could have been put into care for the indigent or into reducing medical costs instead of driving millions into bankruptcy.

The drive back from Romney just before winter solstice, the season's icy teeth snapping in the cold blackness, evokes thoughts of debt and mortality. When you are blue collar and over sixty years old and live in places like historic old Winchester or hard-scrabble Romney, you have many unspoken fears. One of them is winding up in one of these nursing homes. Another is medical bankruptcy long before you are drooling in your peas. Medical bills could siphon off the value of your home while you are still paying for the refinancing you did for earlier medical bills.

Such fears are not unjustified. Like most regional hospitals of its type in the heartland, the Winchester Medical Center is the largest generator of bankruptcies in our area. In general, medical bills are the leading cause of personal bankruptcy in the United States for the uninsured. Half of the uninsured owe money to hospitals, and at any given time one-third of them are being chased by collection agencies that will not hesitate to haul them into court for a hundred bucks. A 2005 Harvard University study found that 50 percent of all bankruptcy filings were wholly or partly the result of medical expenses, a 2,200 percent increase since 1981. The average out-of-pocket medical debt of individu-als who filed for bankruptcy was $12,000. In the United States someone files for bankruptcy every thirty seconds in the after-math of a serious health problem.

All of that is tragic enough, but here's the real irony: Sixty-eight percent of those filing for bankruptcy have health insur-ance. Premiums, deductibles, and uncovered expenses are so high now that the insurance that working people get through their employers does not necessarily save them from financial ruin, especially as they near retirement and experience the health problems that come with age. They often see age sixty as the start of a desperate five-year slog toward the high ground of Social

Security and Medicare, where they can die relatively safe from bankruptcy.

At 9 a.m. on a Saturday, Woody McCauley died the way uncounted Americans do—of massive heart failure while sitting on the toilet. (A bowel movement stresses the system more than you might think.) Two of his grandchildren, ages six and thirteen, were present for the event. The thirteen-year-old, a girl named Alyssa, recalls that Grandpa "roared like a lion" when he died. "It was so scary." Woody was sixty-nine.

His real name was Elwood, but sometime after he came back from the Korean War people started calling him Woody and it stuck. He had spent a year in Korea, where, as he recalled, "I like to got killed and froze several times just so's they could keep a pin in some goddamned map in Washington." After that year of trying to sleep through mortar attacks, the first job he was offered upon return, short-haul truck driver for a grocery distributor, looked so good he kept it for the rest of his life. Health insurance was almost free when he started, though the cost steadily climbed. Woody was satisfied with the job. "I started out at a dollar and a quarter an hour, then went to a salary and got raises over the years. A man without an education can't expect much more than that." He was up to more than $9 an hour when he retired, and he did not consider himself a poor man.

Woody was a diabetic for twenty years before his retirement and had insurance to cover most of his medical expenses. When he became eligible for Medicare, he more or less had the same amount of out-of-pocket expenses; they were just for different things. One month after he crossed the finish line and was getting comfortable with sleeping in until nine, he had a very serious heart attack as well as complications of diabetes, high blood pressure, and a previously undiscovered congenital heart defect. For the next three years or so, he pretty much lived in his bedroom. When he felt well enough, he would listen to old Jim Reeves records, read his annotated Bible, and watch *Buckmasters* and *Texas Deer Hunter* on TV. Though he couldn't hunt anymore, he made sure the guns in his safe were well oiled and polished, just as a Viking might sharpen his sword on the morning of his last day. Then too, he may have been keeping the guns presentable for the day when they would be passed along. In between these activities he'd eat things he wasn't supposed to. Milky Way bars were the worst offenders, though there were others too numerous to mention. But mostly Woody just felt like hell and came out only when the grandkids came over, or to hit the john a dozen times a day thanks to the diuretics.

When Woody returned to his bedroom, there was that bright yellow and black sign on the door that said DO NOT RESUSCITATE—not exactly a pick-me-up. It was a notice to the rescue squad, required by the State of Virginia if you choose not to have tubes rammed down your throat and assorted hardware, taped, glued, and inserted, and electronic beeping and clicking as the last sounds you ever hear. "That glue smell makes me sick on my stomach," he said. In any case, Woody never survived the ambulance ride to the hospital. And if he smelled anything at all before he died, it was the odor of rubber tires burning through ice when the ambulance got stuck in the snow on the potholed

road leading down to his house. But he died in the belief that Social Security and Medicare would take care of his wife Ruth's
basic needs.

Six months later, Ruth, who had been pretty crippled up
herself from spinal disk removals over the past twenty years, was
going nuts from grief and the constant problems with the buck-
ling thousand-square-foot modular home they had almost paid
off. "You work all your life for a house and it don't even last until
you die," she said.

In Ruth's case, "working all your life" added up to fifty-two
years, beginning at the age of fifteen when she convinced the
government she was eighteen so that she could work in the naval
shipyards down in Norfolk with one of her older sisters. After
that it was one factory after another, mostly canning and garment factories, until the left leg began to turn in and atrophy and
she couldn't stand for more than fifteen minutes at a time. So
she "took in kids" to make money, the way people did in the old
days before day care centers. Usually there were about three of
them at any given time, and they cheered her life up quite a bit as
they slurped Kool-Aid and ran around with the family dog on the
grassy acre where the modular was planted.

But now, with Woody gone, it was all just too much. Ruth
thought about selling the house. However, despite the housing
boom, it was the next thing to worthless because no matter how
much you paint "exterior Masonite," it's still glorified cardboard
and goes to hell in under twenty-five years, taking everything
else with it as each winter brings in a little more moisture and
the weight of each winter's snows buckles it a bit more. And the
acre of land was worth next to nothing as a prospective site for

new homes because the septic had never really been "perked" (the original seller knew how to get around percolation tests). New zoning laws were steering development away from that side of the county and toward land owned by speculators who had pull with the county board of supervisors, which meant water and sewer were never going to come to Woody's acre. That made it essentially a useless patch of agricultural land with a shack on it. America's much-touted prosperity surges miss more Americans than they hit, though you'd never know it to read the newspapers. The local business and lifestyle sections always quote and photograph the winners, not the losers.

So Ruth was stuck there until further notice, watching her oil heat bills rise in winter and the cost of air-conditioning go up in the summer and the place fall apart, and waiting for her son to find time to mow the half acre of weeds that was once a lawn. From then on out, Ruth would have to live on $756 a month from Social Security and hope that Medicare held up. This was the security produced by more than half a century of labor.

Theoretically, she had enough to get by. Her monthly bills came to about $645, which she budgeted as follows:

$200 . . . . . . mortgage payment
$160 . . . . . . food
$40 . . . . . . utilities
$65 . . . . . . Plan B Medicare payment
$75 . . . . . . average heating oil bill
$40 . . . . . . phone
$65 . . . . . . high blood pressure medicine

That left $111 for clothing, dentures and dental care, eye examinations and glasses, medical checkups and tests, and a raft of other things. In the best of times the budget would be a precarious little boat to keep afloat. All it took was a worn-out oil furnace to torpedo the boat. Another $300 a month in Social Security would have changed everything. She had paid in enough to easily justify another $500 a month. But she couldn't have done the math, and she wasn't going to get it anyway, because Social Security is a raw deal for most women who have worked and paid into it all their lives.

The trouble is that the program was designed to serve 1930s-style households, where two-thirds of wives stayed home while their husbands worked. Yet nowadays, only one in five wives stays home, and two-thirds of couples are "dual earners," most likely because it takes two jobs to pay for housing, or to live the Martha Stewart pie-in-the-sky lifestyle—or at least nibble around its edges. You might think that a woman who retires after punching the time clock and paying into Social Security year after year would come out better, or at least not worse, than a stay-at-home wife who has hit retirement age. You would be wrong, though: Married working women who pay Social Security taxes receive no more benefits from Social Security than women who have never paid a dime into the program.

Here's how it plays out: A stay-at-home wife who retires can claim "spousal benefits" amounting to 50 percent of the benefits of her husband. The system treats her decently because it was created in 1935, when her situation was the norm. The married working woman has a choice when she retires: She can claim benefits based on her own lifetime earnings or she can choose the spousal benefit, whichever is higher. More likely than not, because she earned less than her husband, she will choose to claim half of her husband's benefits—the same benefit as the married woman who didn't work. So Ruth—and countless other women like her—has paid a mountain of payroll taxes over the years without getting much in return. Researchers at the National Center for Policy Analysis have come up with some startling numbers: "If the second spouse in a couple comprised of two high school–educated twenty-five-year-olds enters the workforce and works full-time, the couple's expected lifetime taxes increase 74 percent, but their benefits will increase only 17 percent."

Older women depend on Social Security more than men. For one thing, their numbers are greater: They represent 67 percent of all people drawing Social Security, 27 million altogether. Twenty-four million of them live entirely on a Social Security check that is often below the official poverty level, especially those entering the program after living their entire lives below the poverty level. Only 13 percent of older women who draw Social Security have additional income, such as pensions, and most who do are from the top 20 percent of Americans in terms of income. I started to write: "And if they do have pensions, they are usually smaller than men's . . ." but realized that pensions are a moot point for working folks in towns like this. No one ever got a pension for coring apples on a canning line or driving a short-haul grocery truck.

Whether you are a man or a woman, Social Security is the most important ongoing domestic story in America. It directly affects tens of millions of American lives. But only when a slow news day comes along—when Britney Spears doesn't strap her baby's car seat in backwards or a bigger and better car bomb doesn't go off in Baghdad—do the media pay attention to Social Security. On such days, pundits, news anchors, and financial analysts tell us that there is a "solvency crisis," that time is running out, and that it will take "political courage" for members of Congress to "agree on a solution to the crisis." None of those pronouncements, however, has much to do with the real issue.

Anyone who bothers to read more than the overheated quotes in the news knows that although a fiscal threat is looming, it is quite a few years off and can be managed. The debate between Democrats and Republicans is not a search for a "bipartisan compromise" but rather an ideological grudge match that began when President Franklin D. Roosevelt first launched the program, mostly to put the lid on a national crisis (riots had begun). Ever since then, bitter conservative ideologues have taken their shots at destroying Social Security: first Alf Landon in 1936, followed by scores of other conservatives with the balls to attack America's most popular program, among them Barry Goldwater and Milton Friedman. Social Security creates moral weakness and dependency, the conservatives argue. It removes the need for discipline, the basis of all that is moral, they say. The fact that if they could commandeer all that Social Security money and pump it through their own enterprises, they would get even richer never comes up. Meanwhile, the Democrats, publicly at least, stick to Roosevelt's "pay it backward" philosophy: Let the fortunate help the unfortunate, let each generation help the previous one find ease and rest in old age, and to hell with the survival-of-the-fittest private investment stuff.

In all those years there has never been compromise because ideology does not by its nature lend itself to compromise. Privatization was merely the latest attempt at grabbing the money, this one wearing a happy face and promising working Americans that they too could make more money by playing the markets just like the big dogs. Once again, the Republicans got the starch blown out of their shorts. Luckily for them, their attempt seems to have gone down the memory hole, and they may never pay a political price for it. They can go back to sawing juicy pieces off Medicare and resume their ideological stewing, leaving Dottie to wonder where the little village hospital went and Ruth to drown in poverty with a cheap oil furnace tied around her neck.

Given that Ruth could not get much for the house anyway, she sold it to her son, Robert, a construction worker, for $5,000. The reasoning behind the decision was good: He would fix the worst of the problems, build another house on the property later, then tear down the old one. Meanwhile, Ruth could stay in her house and pay off the furnace and other bills that had accumulated.

Unfortunately, fate stepped in to give her a kick in the chest. Ruth had serious congestive heart failure, from which she never recovered fully, and it left her needing much more attention than any of her kids, working full-time, could give. Then came the dreaded fall in the kitchen, after which she lay on the floor for eight hours waiting for her son to stop by on his way home from work.

Ruth didn't break a hip, but doctors said there was strong evidence that she had had a stroke and that it looked as though an assisted living facility or even full-time care was in order. But there are few assisted living facilities around here, despite the need for them, and at three grand a month, well . . . A private nursing home at $5,000 a month was even less of an option. For working-class people, the $2,000 spread between the two options makes no difference. Anything over $400 a month, even split between the two children, may as well be a million dollars. If there was going to be care, it would have to be in a facility that accepts Medicare.

Most nursing homes have only a limited number of Medicare beds. Competition for them is keen and involves lots of paperwork, then getting on a waiting list. Ruth got lucky, if you can call it luck. Enough old people died that she got a bed in fewer than two months.

The fact that Ruth was still ambulatory and had most of her marbles was a serious drawback. Nursing homes cannot get funding for people who are likely to do just as well in assisted living, which is too expensive for working people and seldom available in places like this. Consequently, the family had meetings with doctors and with a care center manager, and, after some creative paperwork, it was determined that Ruth had dementia. The family would have to pay a couple hundred dollars a month in addition to what Medicare paid, but everyone breathed a sigh of relief. She was in.

The dementia route is often the easiest way in for families desperately needing access to elder care before a parent breaks a hip or drops a lit cigarette butt into the open drawer of the dresser late at night one more time, as my mother did. Most others in our situation have a similar story.

Ruth's children and grandchildren visited her regularly, and, like so many of the residents suffering from Alzheimer's or damaged by a stroke, she always begged them to get her out of there. The difference between Ruth and the poor old soul down the hall who drifted into Ruth's room and cussed her out for hiding her long dead husband from her was that Ruth knew she had done no such thing and that she was not demented. And week after week she put forward her case for not being demented to her children. But the family was forced to ignore her pleadings because there was no alternative for her care. Everybody felt just plain wrung out after a visit. Even bringing Ruth home for Christmas was no fun—all she did was cry—and as time went on the children cut visits down to a minimum to avoid the sad experience.

One of the things no one thought of when they got Ruth admitted was that if you enter a nursing home on the grounds of dementia, you are likely to be treated for dementia. Ruth was set up with a pharmaceutical treatment progam, and as time passed she got weirder, eventually refusing to do the long hall walks that were the main element in the center's fitness regime. "I don't want all those people grabbing at me and mumbling," she said. It was true enough. It seems that the more addled residents are in these places, the more likely they are to roam the hallways. Increasingly, Ruth stayed in bed, losing body strength and mobility and getting spacier by the month.

Now her children don't feel so guilty. Her daughter Carol says, "It was a good thing she was in the nursing home when she started to go downhill. The timing turned out to be right."

I cannot help but think of Dottie, whose life is thumping along in four-four time these days. Dottie sings at the Dairy Queen once a week backed up by a full five-piece country string band of geezers. "I had to do something about the loneliness of living in an assisted living unit," she tells me. The Dairy Queen is completely filled when she and the band play back near the bathroom door, and a writer from the newspaper even came and did a story on the lady on oxygen who sings.

Dottie says: "It ain't easy dragging that tank down there, but nothing is easy. You have to fight to win. If you see something to do that will move you just one little inch, you have to push to make that inch. That's how you win. I may not have had a long life, but I've had a big life. I've been to New York and to Florida. And when I die, I want to die at the mike. If you happen to be there, I want you to stand up and cheer."

Here we have two women who spent their entire lives working and paid their share of taxes into the till without complaint. One lived an utterly conventional life and was rendered senseless by the system's way of dealing with old people. The other refused to let her soul be trapped in the process. But they are both profit centers in the machinery of a vast system indifferent to their welfare. Neither Dottie nor Ruth will ever hear the artificial debates on Capitol Hill about Social Security and Medicare, the two programs that govern the lives of the 53 percent of Americans with no retirement income other than Social Security.

Half the nation depends entirely on the government for help when they grow old. They paid in advance for that help.

A far larger number will find themselves in America's hospitals and will expect those hospitals to put health and healing before all else. But when our sprawling medical system sees its purpose as seizing market share instead of curing people, and when our elected officials use the most serious domestic issue on the table to settle long-standing ideological grudges, you've got to ask if such a system can even be redeemed, much less reformed.

Ours is a system that destroys the fabric of working-class families' relationships with their elders. The guilt is tremendous. I haven't visited my mother in many months, and when I do visit, she still begs, "Joey, get me out of here." Then she turns her wheelchair, fishes another cigarette out of her pack, and stares into the hallway, each of us condemned to the knowledge that it will never happen.

8

American Hologram

THE APOCALYPSE WILL BE TELEVISED

Bobby Fulk, millionaire realtor, sits in the back booth of Royal Lunch waiting for his burger and fries. The newspaper lies on the table in front of him. Sixtyish, jowly, and red faced, he is well dressed in a dark gabardine sports coat and beige cashmere turtleneck. The best description of what he is doing with that newspaper is "looking at it." You certainly couldn't call it reading because he just scans the headlines. Bobby can't read in any meaningful sense of the word. He has never purchased a book from a bookstore and probably has never read a book on real estate. He doesn't even read the real estate ads in the paper because he has access to the MLS (Multiple Listing Service) on the Internet in his office, and his secretary prints out the listings for him. Presented with a newspaper, he sucks in the headlines as complete summaries of the text: COUNTY REPORTS 7 HOMICIDES THIS YEAR (nobody he knows, so who cares?); BUSH STANDS FIRM ON OPERATION IRAQI FREEDOM (good man, everybody needs freedom, Bobby thinks to himself); and DEVELOPER APPLIES FOR NEW PUD [Planned Unit Development] (he knew the planned development was in the works six months ago). If there's a story about a local high school football or basketball game, he might wade through the first few paragraphs, but only because he's looking for the score.

Bobby is one of the 89 million to 94 million American adults—nearly half of the U.S. adult population—who are functionally illiterate. According to the National Institute for Literacy, they "lack a sufficient foundation of basic [literacy] skills to function successfully in our society." Of these, 17 percent to 20 percent can read just a little. That means that they cannot fill out job applications, understand food labels, or read simple stories to their children. Another 25 percent can read, but not well enough to follow five consecutive paragraphs of text or dense documents such as sales contracts. Bobby Fulk knows the meaning of terms common to most real estate contracts, both from drilling them into his head by watching the training videos he used to pass the realtor's examination and from repeated usage. He is sort of a key-word man—he has learned the key words he needs for his business. He could never write a full contract, but then, residential realtors don't have to. As for any aspects uncommon to the industry's rote residential contracts, the client's lawyers take care of those.

The truth is that Bobby made most of his money by buying very cheap and undesirable residential properties and hanging on to them by renting them out for twenty or thirty years until the real estate boom paid off like a slot machine. The real estate license simply offered more opportunities in the game he played. When it became obvious he was pretty damned well-off, people attributed his success to his "real estate office downtown," which did far more managing of his rental properties than it did buying and selling real estate in most of those years, until he sold the rentals. Bobby didn't need literacy to collect the rent, just a sharp eye for the going rates and a firm attitude about collecting. As to the real estate deals, being astute was as good as being book smart.

Of course there is more to literacy than reading words. In our culture it helps to be able to contextualize an infomercial, not to mention Tom DeLay's crimes. Almost none of the Royal Lunch crowd, however, even knows who Tom Delay is. They do not watch the national news unless the United States attacks somebody or there is a flood in New Orleans. Even if they took the trouble to read George Orwell's *Animal Farm,* none of them would see it as anything other than a story about animals.

In our culture there is also the need to interpret legions of symbols and acronyms (IBM, CBS, GM, FBI, CIA, OBM, MCI, FEMA, HUD . . .) that turn up every day in advertising, product packaging, corporate brochures, government pamphlets, and news stories. Functional illiterates, however, cannot separate industry from government, or the news from an advertisement or an infomercial. Hence the inability of Carolyn (the old flame I bumped into in the Food Lion parking lot) to tell a nonprofit charity from a quick-buck manufacturer of magnetic yellow ribbons. From inside the American hologram an eagle is an eagle and a yellow ribbon is a yellow ribbon. Uneducated and trapped within the hologram, people like Carolyn and Bobby will never be capable of participating in a free society, much less making the kinds of choices that preserve and protect one, unless the importance of full literacy can somehow be made clear to them.

The problem is, they are pretty happy the way they are. Television and movies pump in enough entertainment to give them something to talk about—when they are not debating whether the food at Olive Garden is better than the food at Outback Steakhouse. And most of their friends and family are just like them (they are not rebels raised by philosophy scholars), so they don't often rub up against a different way of looking at things.

Bobby is one of a number of prosperous people here in Winchester who falls into this category, proving that America truly is a land of opportunity. They include car dealers, government construction contractors, and wholesale food distributors who hire people to read and count for them when necessary. Nearly all of these successful folks have made it in the business world by sticking with the free market ideal of survival of the fittest over everything else. They believe in giving no quarter, and consequently they are antiunion, pro–death penalty, and pro-war— that is, until they actually feel the war's cost in their own wallets and a big voice coming out of the sky says: *You could grab more money if we did not have this war to pay for!* This is America, where greed is christened "drive" and is deemed a virtue. Are these successful but unlettered people functioning in society? No. They are functioning in the economy, which to these driven citizens *is* society. "Own more stuff" and "Gain and hold territory" are their only imperatives.

Anyone who thinks that these white conservatives, both working class and small business class, don't care about anything outside their own zone of ignorance is only half right. The fact is that many of them cannot see outside that zone at all. They are too uneducated, too conditioned to the idea that being a consumer is the same thing as being a citizen. (Owning stuff, after all, is lots more fun than exercising the duties of citizenship and, according to our president, is the most patriotic aspect of citizenship.) As we liberals now begin to inveigh against the loss of personal freedoms in the new corporate American state, a much larger freedom has already been lost: the freedom from ignorance.

So long as Pootie, Nance, Dottie, and even Bobby Fulk remain incapable of reading or grasping what the greatest minds have learned and written, or can't tell the difference between a patriotic country song and political truth, we aren't likely to make much human progress, no matter how good the economy is or how much stuff we own. To do that, we are going to have to switch off the hologram before economic collapse, Peak Oil, or the rest of the world does it for us.

Self-expression, the way we recognize ourselves as human beings among other human beings, was once messy and unpredictable, reflecting the assumption that each person is unique. Individuals had to find their own places in society without many clues and not the slightest shred of a "lifestyle" to cling to. For young people self-discovery was full of experiment and error. They had to figure out on their own whether they were leaders, religious, exciting or dull, attractive or at least stomachable, or perhaps homosexual, and how their unique selves fit among their peers at a new school where other unique selves wanted to pound their asses on the playground. How they did it without today's props is a mystery. No nerd duds, preppy shirts, gang-banger shorts, or even a cell phone. No Burton, Vans, Braun,

Nokia, Foot Locker, Oakley, Spy Optics, Salomon, Reebok, Levi Strauss, American Eagle, O'Neill Europe, PlayStation, Hasbro, Columbia Sportswear, Warped Tour.

Neither our fathers, grandfathers, nor we had to "navigate the fast-moving youth landscape" that youth marketers assure kids today they cannot traverse without at least a No Fear baseball cap, a repro vintage dinner jacket, and rugged safari shorts—all worn together and purchasable at the mall. The hologram generates tens of thousands of such social identity keys. Having mixed and matched his newly purchased identity to his satisfaction, that kid photodigitizes it into yet another simulacrum on a camera phone and shoots it into the ionosphere to be downloaded by a similar creature gazing at the same hologram.

The difficulties of self-expression having been neatly eliminated through standardization, adult yokels and urban sophisticates can choose from a preselected array of possible selves based solely on what they like to eat, see, wear, hear, and drive. Your baby can wave from her $400 car seat in the Volvo, perhaps drawing an observer close enough to see the "Pacifist's Pledge" imprinted on her 100 percent hemp T-shirt. When enough of your own kind coagulate around anything, you have a "lifestyle" on your hands. If nothing jells around your own assembled coolness, then you join some larger lifestyle. A thousand magazines give directions on how to do it: *Elle, Savvy Senior, Today's Black Woman, Trailer Life, Harper's Bazaar, Cabin Life, Town and Country,* and, for the affluent, *Grand* (a magazine for well-heeled grandparents), not to mention good ole *High Times.*

The choices are die-cut but seemingly infinite: One woman expresses her fuzzy, warm, and nurturing side by collecting overpriced Care Bears; her husband expresses his manly wildness through his ATV and camo casual wear or his souped-up home computer (the new white boy's hot rod). Meanwhile, farther up the literacy scale, many thousands of would-be writers display their tragically unrecognized wit and insight as movie critics, using mass-distributed blogging software on mass-produced computer hardware to illuminate mass-distributed films (the prevailing assumption being that an audience, however small, is proof enough of authenticity and individuality). They sound like a motley bunch, but they share one modern characteristic: Not one of them made up his or her identity from scratch.

We have come a long way since the days when millions of Americans were concerned with actualizing individual potential, looking inward and asking themselves, "What do I have to offer the world, and how do I become that person?" During the sixties in particular, an optimistic generation made tremendous efforts toward the realization of each American's unique talents and abilities. College doors were thrown open to blacks, to other minorities, and to poor whites previously excluded. There was such vigorous electricity in the air, so many possibilities in ourselves and in America, that this working-class boy grabbed his wife one day and said: "Let's grab the baby and head west, and grow our brains and hearts, read Rilke and Chief Joseph and Rimbaud and Lao-tzu and burn meat on open fires with cowboys! Maybe even meet Allen Ginsberg!" And we did it too. That was before we settled for providing just enough growth opportunities for the working class to render them capable of stocking the shelves of Wal-Mart's fluorescent caverns on the night shift.

These days, working-class Americans are conditioned to respond not as individuals whose opinions may differ radically from the opinions of their neighbors, but as the property of the government. They are conditioned to be, as essayist Lewis Lapham wrote, "happy villagers glad to wave the flags and wage the wars, grateful for the good fortune that placed them in the care of a sublime leader." They aren't "unified by any particular text, but are conditioned in a habit of mind and thinking." They subscribe to no political doctrine as such. Rather, they are bathed, hour after hour, in the televised imagery of the new corporate state, in which eagles scream gloriously above the wreckage of the World Trade Center, in which the enemy is smitten on foreign shores, in which thrilling cavalcades of heavily armed motorcycle police and marching SWAT teams appear larger than life. Ignorant and sated people are not chilled by such sights on their television screens. Far from it.

Liberal or conservative, the average American spends about one-third of his or her waking life watching television. The neurological effects are profound. For example, researcher Herbert Krugman famously demonstrated that television viewing makes the right brain hemisphere twice as active as the left, releasing a surge in the body's natural opiates—endorphins, including beta-endorphins and enkephalin, all of which act on the same brain receptors as opiates. Other research shows suspension of critical-thinking skills. Meanwhile, we watch television pleasurably, believing we understand what we have watched, believing we are always in control of the experience and are not unduly influenced by it.

In truth, television drives the hologram, creates Americans' reality, regulates our national perceptions and interior hallucinations of who we Americans are—the best and the bravest, the richest and the most powerful, the freest country on the planet. Television promotes the illusion du jour, whether it be the environment-destroying automobile as a God-granted entitlement of all Americans, or the reason the United States was *forced* to drop the atomic bomb on Hiroshima, or why Americans, only 6 percent of the world's population, are entitled to use up a quarter of its resources. Television displays menus: sometimes national political candidates preselected by more powerful forces, sometimes consumer goods (perhaps one day the two will merge).

Because our consciousness is entirely based in our brain neurology and neurochemistry, and because television is the one voice and one image projected to the many, it regulates the seasons of our national consciousness. Football season arrives through the screen with its competitive passions, as do election seasons, the Christmas shopping seasons, and especially marketing seasons, with the release of new lines of cars, summer movies, and seasonal clothing lines. The nation's economic life is so dependent on media that many experts now deem ours the "attention economy," given that the numbers of eyeballs focused on TV screens and computer screens are everything these days. Television regulates the national mood, stirring patriotic passion during wars and anxious vigilance against the threat of unseen terrorists, and television responds to the attack on the World Trade Center with the message "Keep on buying," issued from the president's own lips.

A media-generated belief system functions as the operating instructions for society. Television shows us how successful people supposedly behave, invest, and relate to each other. Through crime shows it demonstrates what will happen if we don't behave. Television shows us what an awful place the world supposedly is. Like clockwork, there is the nightly bloodletting through televised wars and domestic murders, interspersed with detective Lenny Briscoe finding corpses at 7, 8, and 11 p.m. weekdays. Television shows us whom we should hate (Hugo Chávez and Fidel Castro, for starters). Anything outside of its parameters represents fear and psychological free fall. Anything outside of it is dirty, unpredictable, incomprehensible, and pocked with risk and tragedy.

Of course millions of Americans do not completely succumb to the hologram, mostly as a result of a true higher education, especially in the arts and humanities. They are capable of understanding that the tragedy of a million deaths in the Sudan or the destruction of the planet's atmosphere are just as real and possibly more important than a Redskins game or this week's special at Popeye's (although Popeye's does make some damned good biscuits). Yet scarcely one in fifty working-class Americans understands this.

But it is not they who are responsible for the slow dismantling of our educational system that has taken place under both Republican and Democratic administrations. The people who have gained the most from that system are the most to blame for its destruction, particularly the upper middle class and the affluent suburban classes that serve the administrative needs of the empire—its commissars, lawyers, public accountants, and stock brokers. These are the catering classes, the men and women whose identity is granted them by the corporation, the brand for which they work. After all, it is the brand that makes possible the accumulation of goods that confer their social standing and ensure they will never be forced to drink tap water or live in a modular home like Nance. In much the same way that old-line fascists dutifully served the state, so the catering classes, both liberal and conservative, serve the brutal American brand of market capitalism. Without them, none of it could possibly work. That's why they must be purchased at a higher rate than the proles. They are more to blame because there are more of them, and between them they have the only true power of revolt. No one would dare openly crush them (even though they too are quietly being weakened). Blame the ruling class? The ruling class is too obvious, too easy. We all see them, even though they are unseeable.

That anyone in the laboring classes sees anything at all is a sheer miracle, given what passes for news reporting. The once noble craft of Ida Tarbell and Edward R. Murrow is now in the hands of praise-seeking pawns of corporate media, drawn from the middle and upper classes. From their narrow, protected vantage point, they can imagine only two kinds of societal stories: (1) worshipful portrayals of the rich, famous, and politically powerful, and (2) tearful glamorizations of crack whores and illegal immigrants. These are the kinds of stories that entertain or stir the emotions of the middle class but do not threaten the status quo. The men and women who produce these stories have no more clue that they have been brainwashed than do the poor working slobs. And if they did know, they might not care because they are comfortable enough and even a bit glamorous.

Republican or Democrat, this nation's affluent urban and suburban classes understand their bread is buttered on the corporate side. The primary difference between the two parties is that the Republicans pretty much admit that they grasp and even endorse some of the nastiest facts of life in America. Republicans honestly tell the world: "Listen in on my phone calls, piss-test me until I'm blind, kill and eat all of my neighbors right in front of my eyes, but *show me the money!* Let me escape with every cent I can kick out of the suckers, the taxpayers, and anybody else I can get a headlock on, legally or otherwise." Democrats, in contrast, seem content to catalog the GOP's outrages against the Republic, showing proper indignation while laughing at episodes of *The Daily Show.* But they stand behind the American brand: imperialism. They "support our troops," though you will be hard put to find any of them who have served alongside them or who would send one of their own kids off to lose an eye or an arm in Iraq. They play the imperial game, maintain their credit ratings, and plan to keep the beach house and the retirement investments if it means sacrificing every damned Lynndie England in West Virginia.

The trouble is that consuming like this provides no sense of accomplishment—not for the corporate class or for any other. You don't get the satisfaction that comes of having created something. You don't experience the pleasing disorientation of connecting with another person. Consuming just breeds frustration—that is, until you imbibe enough Prozac to feel comfortable shopping again. But no matter how much junk this corporation called America can stuff into its laboring class, there is still the basic foundation of oppression that characterizes working-class life but is never acknowledged. If you live with it, you keep it stuffed inside. If you are not one who lives close to it and feels it, you cannot see it. Well-off suburban and urban professionals see only the fakeries concocted by the corporate media, the entertaining and offensive likes of David Spade's Joe Dirt bad hair losers, or Viacom's country music specials based on the families of "our fighting eagles in Iraq." And the very people who should be most insulted by all this absorb and believe it themselves.

Americans, rich or poor, now live in a culture woven entirely of illusions, and all of us are rendered actors. Television actors portray nonactors in "reality shows," and nonactors in Congress perform in front of the cameras, grappling over the feeding tube in Terri Schiavo. Michael Jackson shows up for court in pajamas, and Jeff Weise shows up for class with a gun.

Social realism in this country is a television commercial celebrating America. The Soviets posterized thick, broad-shouldered women of the steppes cradling sheaves of grain in their arms. We have Kirstie Alley stepping from our TV screens, the Salome of Jenny Craig bearing America-the-Corporate's glad tidings to an obese republic—a simulated republic of eagles, church spires, brave young soldiers and firefighters, and "freedom of choice," a heroic feast within the temple, so long as we do not stray outside the hologram. Which is to say, until the coming economic and ecological collapse.

The corporate simulacrum of life has penetrated us so deeply it has become internalized and now dominates our interior landscape. Just as light pollution washes out the nighttime sky, so much of our day-to-day existence has lost its depth and majesty, having been replaced by constellations of commercial images. So marvelous is their glow that ordinary people will do

the most extraordinary things to be represented in the constella-
tion for a few brief moments—grovel at the zipper of Donald
Trump's trousers, confess to marital infidelities before millions,
and do other completely degrading and unimaginable things.
We are all watching the hologram and cannot see one another in
the breathing flesh. Within the hologram sparkles the culture-
generating industry, spinning out mythology like cotton candy.
We all need it to survive. Hollywood myths, imperial myths,
melting-pot myths . . .

Our culture is based on two things: television and petroleum.
Whether you are Pootie or the president, your world depends on
an unbroken supply of both. So it is small wonder that we all
watch a televised global war for oil as brain-wave entertainment.
As a consequence, we receive the conditioning required to sustain our acceptance of the state brutality occurring at the edges
of the empire in the quest for oil. How much of this convenient
symbiosis linking corporate television, war as a corporate profit
center, and corporate oil was consciously planned we can never
know until we are redeemed from the blinding effects of the
corporate-sponsored hologram.

We live in an age of corporate dominion just as we once lived
in an age of domination by royal families, kings, and warlords.
From inside the hologram there is no history, no memory, no
way to equate the tribute rendered to the credit card companies,
the insurance companies, the IRS, the power cartels, and the home
mortgage banks with the kind of debt bondage they actually

represent. Yet we must pay such tribute to be allowed to survive in our society, even if that tribute is a trailer payment at usury rates or allowing a credit card company access to our medical insurance payment history. We must trade liberty and privacy in increments for comfort and perceived security. That has been the Devil's bargain from the beginning. If middle-class Americans do not feel threatened by the slow encroachment of the police state or the Patriot Act, it is because they live comfortably enough and exercise their liberties very lightly, never testing the boundaries. You never know you are in prison unless you try the door.

America's much-ballyhooed liberty is largely fictional. Three percent of us are either in the joint playing dress-up with some jailhouse papa or on parole and linked with our vast networks of prisons and proxy jailers via electronic tracking devices. One-quarter of all the prisoners on earth are in American prisons by the hand of their own government. My own beloved wife does not find this particularly disturbing, and far too many of my friends find it comforting. The rest of us are captives of credit, our jobs, our need for health insurance, or our ceaseless quest for a decent retirement fund. A decade ago financial advisers deemed $100,000 adequate for retirement. As of this writing, Kiplinger's says half a million dollars and up. More simply put, you can never have enough money, period.

Every human experience in America is mediated for profit by a middleman or by a sparkling new pleasure technology. The process was accelerated half a century ago when television began to seize the political and intellectual world away from ordinary Americans. Now the pseudo-experience of television has shifted into cyberspace. But is the cyberworld's infinite and abstract universe expanding or contracting? Are we being freed or crushed? We cannot know until it is too late.

Nor can we know from within the hologram's many parallel universes and snow globes about the global reality, much less class reality, unless we experience fleshly encounters with the other humans in our neighborhoods and communities. Now more than ever, the middle class cannot see the working class, and the working class cannot see past the next basketball play-offs. True to the working-class sports-culture aesthetic, they remain spectators to politics, responding to each political play with emotion instead of reason, if they respond at all.

Yes, I have written about unarticulated class anger, anxiety, and insecurity, but these are approximately happy people, thanks to the hologram. When happiness is based completely on the thinnest observable material conditions of life—a new truck in the driveway, an iPod in your pocket, the availability of round-the-clock entertainment—it's easy to be happy. When social conscience extends no farther than ourselves, our friends, and our family, then Darfur or secret American prisons abroad are not a problem. When we wake to a heartland newspaper that assures us that the most important thing going on today is the Winchester Kiwanis pancake breakfast and the county supervisors' debate about the height of a flagpole (the supervisors' patriotic decision will doubtless be "high enough to cold-cock a migrating Canadian goose, because it's our nation's flag by God!"), and when we listen to the local talk radio host's assurances that our country is whipping the bad guys and extending democracy worldwide, and at a profit to boot (but we're gonna need another thirty thousand troops to finish the job), and that we live in the freest nation in the world, well, something resembling happiness pervades our lives.

I guess it is best to end this book where it started, at dusk in Royal Lunch. Much has happened since I began writing this book. For one thing, karaoke night has been discontinued. "People can only listen to so many crummy singers," the owner says. The streetscape, which remained unchanged for almost a hundred years, changed recently. Suburban growth out there in cupcake land has been such that a fancy brew pub opened here in the old downtown area, half a block from Royal Lunch in the old grocery warehouse next to the train station. I want to be there when Pootie goes over to investigate what a six-dollar beer tastes like. He's unavailable right now though, because he has become a "watermelon broker." So Poot is down in Florida "putting together a load," which he will sell off the back of a flatbed alongside the road. "There's real money in melons," he swears. But I don't see how, given that watermelons are so cheap they are smashed alongside the road for half a mile to announce to tourists that they are approaching a roadside truck selling them.

Unsurprisingly, during the time I spent on this book, Mary Golliday died. Also, Dottie's health has deteriorated to the point where she must have oxygen round the clock and a noisy machine generating it in her bedroom, distributing it through a plastic tube long enough to reach clear into downtown Romney, from the looks of it. But Dottie still hammers on, carrying her oxygen tank and five spares in the back of her car, which she's driving again. Last week she sang at a club near the West Virginia line. She did it sitting down. "I was afraid the audience would hear the oxygen coming through the nasal canula, so I yanked it off and stopped for breath after every line." She got a standing ovation, not out of pity but out of respect for her courage. Dink Lamp, the fellow who whipped the chimpanzee at the carnival, got born-again—again. Near as I can tell, this is the third time. Even from within the grip of Christ, even without karaoke night at Royal Lunch, he's kept his musical career together and sings hymns at the old folks' homes in a modified version of his previous style. Last I saw of him, he was singing at the nursing home where my mother lives. He closes with Charlie Daniels's "This Ain't No Rag, It's a Flag." I think this Iraq War, now that it's hopelessly lost, has finally gotten even Dink worked up, at least musically.

Right now in this dimming light and waning empire, Royal Lunch is a pinpoint in the hologram. And as the streetlights come on, the bartender reads aloud a *Washington Times* editorial:

> Americans make lousy imperialists. We don't do Nuremberg rallies. Americans make pretty good soldiers, as a lot of men in Valhalla could tell you, but when the shooting stops the American GI only wants to come home, marry the girl next door, pop the top on a cool one and watch the Patriots clock the Eagles. It's what makes him distinctively American. So here's another round of heartfelt applause for the lousy imperialist: This Bud's for you.

A couple of heads nod appreciatively. Outside, police car lights are flashing as cops search a teenager for dope. The young cops act like characters they've seen in crime dramas, and the preacher inside the full Gospel Church is speaking in tongues. *Aba laguila babklon hamalia gero landomomni.* Down the tracks by the train station comes the approaching rumble of the C&X. *Bloooooonk! Bloooooooooonk!* goes its air horn. I think back to 1960, when I sold papers on this corner, and I remember the crying young Greek in the kitchen. Now the police car lights bounce off the storefront windows, and there is the smell of beer and the past and a sure enough approaching apocalypse, and the whole damned sad hologram of America rises up, arching over the laboring millions who sustain the juggernaut of armaments and jet boats and condos and Corfam countertops. And the face on the flickering TV screen recites "today's numbers." Employment numbers and the number of Americans killed in Iraq and stock market numbers slosh against the beaches of awareness alongside the football scores and the number of cockroaches swallowed by a busty blonde on *Fear Factor,* meaningless numbers that, like the cops outside and the drinkers inside, were long ago lost beneath the hologram's gushing spectacle.

ACKNOWLEDGMENTS

As my editor Rachel Klayman says, I am an undeniable product of the Internet. It was an act of desperation. After three decades of writing in the magazine and newspaper business, I was very frustrated with magazines and newspapers and tired of the glib paint-by-number material that clogged the newsstands in the never-ending search for the broadest demographic upon whom to inflict advertising. By 2002, I had said the hell with it, it's easier to mindlessly edit meaningless copy, take home a paycheck, and have health insurance. By then the Internet had grown up while no one in the publishing industry was looking, and it was providing a democratic format that would allow for real diversity of expression and completely unique ideas—an opportunity for a writer to say exactly what he wanted the way he wanted to say it, and let the readers decide for themselves without the intervention of the print industry's editorial drones, of which I was one.

I had no idea how to submit material to the Internet. It was a different animal entirely. So I just e-mailed a couple of pieces to sites whose content seemed to deal with the same American and global issues that had begun to plague the minds of millions of Americans who held the same liberal views. I sent them to counterpunch.org and energygrid.org, not expecting much to happen. A couple of days later, when my e-mail box filled up completely with intelligent responses such as I seldom saw in the magazine trade, and one of the webmasters later told me I had reached several million like-minded readers in a single month, I could have cried for joy. At last there was an alternative. No magazine, not even the largest, could have accomplished such numbers or allowed such freedom.

For providing that alternative and helping me understand Internet culture, I must thank Jeffrey St. Clair at counterpunch .org, both for putting my essays before millions and for demonstrating that the Internet was, among many things, the scene of a struggle to keep the truth before the public. And I must thank Andrew Paterson in England at energygrid.org for taking a special interest in my working-class viewpoint, clarifying my American style to European readers when necessary. I was soon indebted to others who championed my view that a working-class leftist view is possible and does indeed exist in this country. In Canada there was Tony Sutton at coldtype.net—a brilliant editor and old-hand South African freedom fighter whom I am proud to have publish and illustrate my work and advise me on the subject of gin. Next came Sunil Sharma at dissidentvoice.org/, an Internet son of mine by digital blood who showed me that a love of liberty is alive and well in the next generation. Others include: Bev Conover of onlinejournal.com, who, like so many Net supporters, shared some bleak political times and events, even arising from the sick bed to get my stuff online; Jeff Tiedrich at smirkingchimp.com, whose forum gave me much-needed feedback on my sociopolitical thinking, especially that of Mizz Grizz, whose similar Appalachian roots made her my true compass and best critic; the good people at democraticunderground.com for the same, with special thanks to Wiley White, the "Brokeback Carpet Layer"; Patrice Greanville, cjonline.org, one wise and worldly political thinker who, as a similar sufferer, also helped me learn to cope with my lung disease and be productive at the same time; Katherine Yurica of yuricareport.com, who understood my essays on the neoconservative Christian back when most readers thought I was overestimating their political power; Thomas Baypeyras in France at orbite.info, the first to voluntarily translate my works into a foreign language, with sparkling annotations that help French readers understand such Americanisms as "a peckerwood who doesn't know shit from Shinola."

Among the many other freedom-loving netizens who published and/or stood up to defend my work, or criticize it when necessary, are (in no particular order):

alternet.org • worldnewstrust.com •
peaceandjustice.org • Bartcop.com •
enrevanche.blogspot.com • tinyrevolution.com •
peakenergy.blogspot.com • people.tribe.net •
talk2action.org • fairshot.typepad.com •
happyfeminist.typepad.com • stupidevilbastard.com •
opednews.com • arvinhill.blogspot.com • peakoil.com •
jdeanicite.typepad.com • idleworm.com •
theamericanmuslim.org • wealthbondage.com •
williambowles.info • thehollywoodliberal.com •
adreampuppet.blogspot.com • taylor-report.com •
badattitudes.com • alternativesmagazine.com •
benedictionblogson.com • zionsherald.org •

peacebang.blogspot.com • blog.wirearchy.com •
selvesandothers.org • mickeyz.net • swans.com •
moonofalabama.org • theunknowncandidate.blogspot.com
• thomasmccay.blogspot.com • blondesense.blogspot.com
• unknownnews.net • narconews.com • electricedge.com •
theriverblog.blogspot.com • allspinzone.blogspot.com •
liberalgirlnextdoor.blogspot.com • effwit.blogspot.com •
susiemadrak.com • abigfatslob.blogspot.com

My deepest thanks to my pal Eleanor Cooney, seasoned
author and zen gonzo witch, who took the effort to promote my
work to publishing houses; and to Jennifer Matsui, media/social
critic and Japan's oldest practicing mail-order bride, whose tire-
less wit and encouragement was more appreciated than she can
ever know. Likewise to Neddi Jingo and King of Zembla, just
plain intelligent and aware souls out there on the Net who took
the time to connect with a curmudgeon writer because, well, similar minds run in the same gutter. On a slightly different plane,
my deepest gratitude to physicist and political activist George
Salzman, a true guiding elder and friend. My sincerest thanks to
Frederick Clarkson, author and America's best expert on right-
wing Christian politics, who gave his time to review portions of
this book. Gratitude also to former coworkers Roger Vance, Carl
VonWodtke, and Nan Siegel at Weider History Group for bearing
with me as I held down a more-than-full-time job while trying to
write a book at the same time. And not least to Jim Edmonds and
Larry and Anne Wadsworth, who own the working-class taverns
where so many sons of a toiling God find respite and where parts
of this book take place.

To all of them, my heartfelt gratitude.

And most of all, thanks to my agent, Daniel Greenberg, for his ceaseless efforts on my behalf during a difficult time, and to my editor, Rachel Klayman, who first saw value in my work and spent countless hours teaching a novice the book publishing game.

ABOUT THE AUTHOR

JOE BAGEANT writes an online column (www.joebageant.com) that has made him a cult hero among gonzo-journalism junkies and progressives. He has been interviewed on Air America and comments on America's long history of religious fundamentalism in the BBC/Owl documentary *The Vision: Americans on America.*

Born in Winchester, Virginia, Joe served in the U.S. Navy during the Vietnam era and then moved west, living in communes and hippie school buses in and around Boulder, Colorado. In 1971 he began writing magazine and alternative newspaper articles about countercultural figures such as Allen Ginsberg, Timothy Leary, and Hunter S. Thompson. Very quickly he found himself writing about popular culture, media, and politics for the *Rocky Mountain News, Denver Post,* and other mainstream Western newspapers.

In 1981 he moved to the Coeur d'Alene Indian reservation in Idaho, where he built a cabin on twenty acres, lived without electricity, and worked with horses (what locals there call "stump ranching," because after building a cabin the hard way, one is left surrounded by tree stumps). He tended reservation bar, taught at the tribal school part-time, and wrote for regional newspapers and magazines for several years. He also spent ten years in Eugene, Oregon, working for an international corporation that published agricultural magazines.

Ultimately, like most southerners who write, he had a strong desire to get back to his roots, and he returned to his hometown of Winchester, Virginia. Until recently he worked as a senior editor for the Weider History Group.

Joe and his wife, Barbara, recently downsized their lives in America so Joe could spend half the year in Belize, where he writes and sponsors a small development project with the Black Carib families of Hopkins Village.

Printed in the United States
by Baker & Taylor Publisher Services